KV-236-861

Local Studies and the History of Education

HISTORY OF
EDUCATION SOCIETY

Local Studies and
the History of Education

Edited for the Society by
T. G. COOK

METHUEN & CO LTD
11 New Fetter Lane London EC4P 4EE

First published in 1972
by Methuen & Co Ltd
11 New Fetter Lane London EC4P 4EE

© 1972 by History of Education Society

Typeset by The Pentagon Bureau London
Printed in Great Britain by
Straker Brothers Ltd.,
Whitstable.

SBN 416 76420 7

KINGSTON UPON THAMES
PUBLIC LIBRARIES

J16168

ALL   CLASS 370.942
CR   HIS
CAT   REF
cse   907

220 873-01801

Distributed in the USA by
HARPER & ROW PUBLISHERS, INC.
BARNES & NOBLE IMPORT DIVISION

Contents

History of Education Society

Chairman	David Bradshaw (Principal, Doncaster College)
Vice-Chairman	Professor Brian Simon (University of Leicester)
Secretary	Ian Taylor (St John's College, York)
Treasurer	Trevor Hearl (St Paul's College, Cheltenham)
Editor of the Bulletin	T.G. Cook (University of Cambridge)
Other Committee Members	Professor W.H.G. Armytage (University of Sheffield) Professor Kenneth Charlton (King's College, University of London) Malcolm Seaborne (Principal, Chester College) Nanette Whitbread (City of Leicester College)

The aim of the Society, founded in 1967, is to further the study of the history of education by providing opportunities for discussion among those engaged in its study and teaching.

Conferences and meetings are organized, a bulletin is published twice a year in spring and autumn, a journal, *History of Education*, and other publications pertaining to the history of education are sponsored. Membership is open to all connected in a professional capacity with education, or engaged in the study or teaching of the history of education. Overseas members are welcomed and are offered a specially reduced subscription rate. Libraries are invited to subscribe to the bulletin only; otherwise Society membership is individual not institutional.

Annual subscriptions	Members	£2
	Overseas members (surface mail)	£1
	Student members	50p
	Libraries	£1

Life membership £25

Life membership (overseas) £10

Enquiries about membership of the Society, which is open to all engaged in teaching or studying the subject, should be addressed to the Secretary, Mr Ian Taylor, at St John's College, York, YO3 7EX.

Preface

Provided with substantial conference papers on a theme of current relevance to historians of education, and encouraged by the reception given to earlier volumes of conference papers, there was little doubt that the Committee of the Society would seek to add *Local Studies and the History of Education* to the volumes of papers already published by Methuen and Co: *Studies in the Government and Control of Education* (1970), *The Changing Curriculum* (1971) and *History, Sociology and Education* (1971). The Society is grateful to the speakers at the Sheffield conference for agreeing to the inclusion of their papers in this volume and in certain cases to undertaking to expand their contribution beyond the scope of the paper they gave to the conference. Acknowledgement is also made to the Leicester University Press for agreeing to the inclusion of two of the papers. In each case a note accompanying the contribution to this volume explains its relationship to the publication of the University Press. The Press's Secretary, Mr Peter Boulton, was very helpful in the negotiations.

Robert Douch of the University of Southampton took the chair at the sessions of the Sheffield conference devoted to resources. He readily accepted an invitation to write the Introduction to the volume. In view of his interest in and concern for local studies, it was thought appropriate to suggest that he might use the opportunity for general comment on the theme of the conference as well as particular comments on the individual contributions.

The Society is once again indebted to Methuen and Co for undertaking publication. The Society's Editor acknowledges gratefully the interest shown and help given by Methuen's editorial staff and, in particular, by Mrs Linden Stafford. We are once again grateful to Mr David Hempsall for preparing the index.

T.G. Cook
University of Cambridge

Introduction by Robert Douch

The 1971 Conference of the History of Education Society was held in December at Sheffield University with the theme, 'Local Studies and the History of Education'. The chapters of this book reproduce, substantially as they were delivered, all the papers which were read on that occasion.

The objects and the impact of a book, however, differ in some respects from those of a weekend conference. Some adjustments have therefore been made. The first three chapters which report the results of research that had been recently undertaken by their respective authors are printed in a different order from that in which the papers were originally read. The other four contributions were conceived as shorter papers illustrating some of the possibilities and problems of working with particular types of source materials. Some of the latter have now been extended. It is also worth suggesting that the final chapter, much of which discusses student teachers' work, may usefully be regarded as representing a different area of interest from those which precede it, since it relates to a teaching-learning situation and not to professional academic study.

A brief summary of the contents of the book indicates the nature and variety of the topics considered. Dr J.M. Sanderson of the University of East Anglia traces the activities of 'The National and British Societies in Lancashire 1806-1839' and reveals 'the roots of Anglican supremacy in English education'. Professor A.M. Everitt of the University of Leicester, examining 'Nonconformity in the Victorian countryside', suggests that the distribution of dissent was closely related to certain types of local community all of which, for various reasons, enjoyed an unusual degree of freedom, and he encourages the student of educational history to investigate the implications of his conclusion. M.V.J. Seaborne, Principal of Chester College of Education, assesses an outstanding school architect and his work in 'E.R. Robson and the board schools of London', crediting him with the achievement of integrating both the architectural and educational aspects of school design. In his examination of 'The use of ecclesiastical records', J. Lawson of the University of Hull identifies many valuable and neglected documentary sources of educational significance, especially for the period before 1800. M.E. Bryant of the University of London similarly refers to a whole range of 'Topographical resources' before incorporating evidence from many of them into her account of, and commentary on, 'Private and secondary education in Middlesex from the sixteenth to the nineteenth century'. G.R. Batho of the University of Sheffield also embraces a wide variety of 'Sources for the history of history teaching in elementary schools 1833-1914' and, although he suggests that 'the history of history teaching is a dreary enough story', he is able to find some early examples of good practice. Finally, N. Morris of the University of Manchester, in 'The contribution of local investigations to historical knowledge', isolates one aspect of the involvement of student teachers in local history studies and questions the value of much of their activity.

It is perhaps foolish to base many general observations concerning local studies and the history of education on a collection of papers which is both small and, in some respects, haphazard. Nevertheless, the contents of the present volume do illustrate some of the improvements and some of the difficulties and limitations that characterize recent developments in studies of this kind.

First, the improvements. It is not so long since the history of education tended to be studied in isolation, as if education was little influenced by, and did not itself much influence, society in general. But all these papers illustrate the theme of local studies *and* the history of education, and not simply their significance *in* the history of education. Clearly they are concerned with education as a part of a larger social history. Religion, politics, economics and education are all inextricably interwoven in Dr Sanderson's study, and particular educational outcomes are seen to be buried deep in the social past. The structure of local communities is at the very heart of Professor Everitt's thesis. Mr Seaborne not only places Victorian school design in the setting of Victorian architecture in general, but he also sees Robson as representative of a newly emerging social group, 'the archetype of the new civic official'. Freshest of all perhaps is Miss Bryant's identification of the variety of educational provision in eighteenth- and nineteenth-century Middlesex, manifested in many particular ways to meet the growing and changing personal and vocational needs of suburbia. Much of this provision sprang from below to meet the requirements of certain sections of the community, in sharp contrast to so much of English education which has been provided, for a mixture of motives, from above. In commenting on the educational influence of the eighteenth-century London booksellers she also emphasizes the significance of extra-institutional education, an aspect which does not always attract the attention that it deserves. A fundamental result of ending the isolation of history of education studies is that long-term influences and the continuing interplay of countless people and varied problems replace apparently sudden and isolated 'great events'. Major landmarks do not appear almost from the conjuror's hat, but are appreciated as the often belated, and sometimes distorted, outcome of cross-currents and controversies. Certainly not least important is the increased awareness that what did happen did not inevitably happen, and that a different result or solution might sometimes have been preferable in the long term.

Within this increased complexity the importance of the work of individuals, many of them unrecorded in standard works, stands out. Surely the success of the National Society in Lancashire ultimately owed most to J.B. Sumner, Bishop of Chester and subsequently Archbishop of Canterbury? And how many readers of this book had previously heard of E.R. Robson? We need to reconsider and enlarge our list of the leaders of educational change.

Until recently the types of source material generally used in studying the history of education have been limited. Written sources, especially the records of individual ancient foundations, Acts of Parliament and Reports of Commissions and Committees of Enquiry have figured large. Since 1945 with the general establishment of county and borough record offices, important new materials have become available but have so far not been extensively used. Mr Lawson, drawing chiefly but not solely on the archives of the Borthwick Institute at York, indicates many valuable classes of ecclesiastical record, such as bishops' registers, wills and visitation documents, the counterparts of which will be found all over the country. Likewise Mr Batho utilizes little-explored material in local record offices, including school log-books, pupil-teacher records and children's work-books. He and Miss Bryant also draw attention to neglected material in the Public Record Office. Furthermore, as they show, there is a variety of general source materials, both primary and secondary, to be tapped, some of which like the Taunton Report, though much used already, still have new evidence to offer if different questions are asked of them.

The value to the historian of education of school buildings and their furniture and fittings has been demonstrated on a grand scale by Mr Seaborne in his recent book, *The English School: its Architecture and Organisation, 1370-1870,* and his contribution here on the work of Robson must be seen against that background. Pictorial material, such as etchings, engravings, paintings and photographs, may provide very useful evidence where buildings have been destroyed or altered, and also show the appearance of children, schoolrooms and school occasions at different times in the past. Not much has been systematically gathered and published, though several localities did collect together material of this kind as part of their 1870 Education Act centenary celebrations. Information that can be derived from maps and plans is mentioned only briefly by Miss Bryant and Mr Seaborne. The value of oral evidence is not exemplified, an omission which may be partly explained by the fact that there is little reference to the recent past in these papers.

Local studies in the history of education are sometimes classified, as they are by Mr Lawson at the beginning of his contribution, in two groups. First, there are those which concentrate on a single institution or on provision in an area for its own sake – the pious school histories, the traditional accounts in the Victoria County History, the local education authority handbooks, many theses. There is little or no attempt to relate the story to local life generally or to society at large. Then there are those studies which by recreating the past in various localities seek to verify, modify or revise some assumption or belief concerning national developments. The present studies suggest a third category. Dr Sanderson reveals the interplay of national groups and local communities. Robson's work with the London School Board had repercussions in many different and widespread parts of the country. The development of girls' education and the establishment of proprietary schools in London in the nineteenth century exercised an influence far afield. There are, that is, numerous occasions when local study is interesting and important because of its regional and national links and repercussions.

Examples have now been given to suggest some of the ways in which the papers included in this volume may illustrate recent trends towards a more soundly based approach to local studies involving the history of education. The papers also illustrate some of the problems. A major difficulty for students is the definition of 'local' which will vary with the purpose and nature of particular enquiries. The word may be used in the vague sense of implying the inclusion of an isolated example or two to support an alleged national generalization: frequently, of course, the necessary work has not been undertaken throughout the country as a whole properly to establish the generalization. This problem is often a considerable one since until very recently English educational provision has developed essentially in and from the localities and so the investigator might more usually expect to find differences rather than similarities from place to place. The geographical areas that are covered by different local studies also vary enormously. One author will be concerned with the history of a particular school, another with many schools of a similar type but in different places, yet another with the whole variety of institutions in a specific area. Different administrative units form the basis of study, perhaps a diocese or a parish, or it may be a school board or a local education authority, all of which obviously have very different boundaries. In these circumstances, the building-up of broader pictures, interesting comparisons and significant generalizations is often difficult. Are more forward planning and teamwork desirable and, if they are, how might they be introduced? How do particular researchers at present select the area and topic on which they will work? Ease of access, availability and manageability of records, and personal ties and predilections are among the important factors. To what extent do these result in any significant distortions in our appreciation and understanding of any aspects, trends or developments?

Recent studies, including the present papers, illustrate one noticeable concentration of interest and effort, namely a preponderance of studies relating to the nineteenth century. It would not be difficult to suggest reasons for this; for example, interest in the beginnings of a widespread national provision of elementary and secondary education and the existence of large local and national collections of readily comprehensible documents. But these reasons apply also to the twentieth century, and far less attention is paid to this period. What are the reasons for this? To what extent are they linked with problems of sources or with an attitude towards what is considered to be, or not to be, 'historical'? Another aspect on which relatively little work has been done is the curriculum of schools and other educational institutions — content, methods of teaching, textbooks and resources used, attitudes of teachers and children, and relationships between home and school. Often it is not difficult to discover what was recommended to take place in, for example, a particular kind of school at a certain time; what is not so easy is to find much exemplification of what actually did go on. Comparative studies have likewise been little exploited. How often do historians of local developments in England consider corresponding or contrasting developments in Wales, Scotland or Ireland, to say nothing of venturing further afield? How often even are significant comparisons attempted between different parts of England itself?

This introduction must end here. Perhaps it should have ended sooner since, while the writer heard the authors read their papers and has since reflected on them, they have had no opportunity of commenting on his contribution.

One final point. It is interesting to compare the list of members of the History of Education Society with the list of contributors to this volume. A very large part of the membership consists of teachers in colleges of education. Yet all the contributors are from universities, with the exception of the Principal of Chester College who was himself recently translated from the University of Leicester. Are there important implications in this? And if there are, is one that the Society's activities concentrate too much on the academic study of the history of education by professionals and give insufficient time to the work and problems of students in training? How do their encounters with the history of education contribute to their personal and professional development? Only Mr Morris raises such topics here. Perhaps they should form the theme for a future conference.

MICHAEL SANDERSON

The National and British School Societies in Lancashire 1803-1839: the roots of Anglican supremacy in English education

Scarcely any factor was more important in the shaping of the school system in England in the nineteenth century than religion. It was true that the conflicts between Church and dissent and their entrenched interests could impede the development of a State system in those years and did taint the debate about the reform of public education with an unseemly rancour. And yet the religious hostility of the two sides gave to the extension of elementary education a dynamic and stimulus that it may not have acquired had it been totally the product of some secular consensus. The clash of Church and dissent in this sphere was polarized in the struggle between the two societies for religious education that embodied their views, the National Society for the Church of England, and the British Society which, though starting and remaining ostensibly non-sectarian in intention, came quickly to focus much of the activity of dissent. One of the fundamental troubles of the 'religious question' in nineteenth-century education was the fact that the Church was so much more powerful than its rivals. Accordingly any schemes to raise public money for the support of schools tended to arouse bitter opposition and often to founder on the consequent complaint against non-Anglican money being used to finance Anglican education. While this is well appreciated and recurs as a theme throughout the nineteenth century, what is less explained is exactly why the Anglican National Society was able to gain such a position of supremacy over its British rival that gave it such a commanding position to take the fullest benefit of State finance from the 1830s. It is the purpose of this paper to try to throw light on this conflict and on its uneven character. Moreover since many of these issues can only be appreciated through their working-out at the local level and since this conference is specifically concerned with the theme of the application of local studies, the matter will be approached through a close consideration of the rivalry of the British and National Societies in the county of Lancashire. This was an area which had an obviously special economic and social importance at this time, and in which dissent was quite active, and for both these reasons the Church paid it particular attention. It is thus not merely an illustrative local example but the battle ground in which one of the contending parties had the strategic insight to see that a decisive victory could be won over its opponent.

I

There were pressing reasons why it was desirable to create these societies for day education in the 1810s and to expand them in the next two or three decades. In the first place there is some evidence that although the literacy rates for most of England were rising throughout the later eighteenth and early nineteenth centuries yet those for Lancashire were declining [1], and few people realized this better than the clergymen in whose registers the illiterate scrawled crosses came increasingly to replace the written name. This situation was largely attributable to those familiar economic and social changes at work in the north of England stemming from the rising population and the demands of child work leading to a decline in day education and a rise in less satisfactory part-time substitutes. All these created deficits in day-school education whose importance after a period of neglect had to be reasserted. In particular, industrialization created new, growing, poorly paid communities often in remote areas without social and cultural facilities or in rapidly expanding towns whose extremities were filled with populations far in excess of what could be catered for by existing means. Writing on behalf of Bottom Gate in 1824 and appealing for funds from the National Society a clergyman wrote, 'the population around Blackburn is very much scattered and is found in large masses at most inconvenient distances from the central National School' [2], and at Great Marsden in the 1830s a school was needed to cope with the needs of factory hands 'suddenly located here by the capricious spread of manufactures' [3]. Such situations and such demands were but typical of dozens of letters to both the British and National Societies at the time.

None of the Christian bodies either Anglican or nonconformist could continue with equanimity to let this situation deteriorate, for what was at stake was not merely the mechanical skills of literacy nor even social stability but the paramount issue of the salvation of souls. There is a certain tendency in our more secular age to regard elementary education in the early nineteenth century as a middle-class ideological exercise in the social control and discipline of the lower orders to reconcile them to the rigours of urban industrial society. It is salutary to remember that the crusade was nothing so mundane as this. One Lancashire clergyman described his children as 'a tribe of embryo angels training for the skies' [4], another told his scholars with stern logic that if they persisted in shuffling about then God would not love them, and if they died without his love 'you will be punished in hell with the devil . . . for years without end' [5]. If these quotations now seem either amusing or repellent it may be our loss that we cannot fully appreciate the emotional intensity and deadly seriousness of the men who uttered them and the attitudes to education that they and their kind represented. This conscience-driven urgency was the dynamic behind the education of religious bodies rather than any more calculating approach to social engineering. This stress on Christianity as the centre of education led indeed to the view held by two important figures in the Lancashire National Society movement, Bishop Blomfield and the Rev. Horace Powys, that secular education without religion was in fact more productive of evil than good [6]. The National and British Societies had not only their Christianity in common but also their Protestantism and this gave them yet another motive for education. As deists formed their religious beliefs through reason, the Enthusiasts through illumination and the Ritualists through oral precept so the Protestants both Anglican and nonconformist based their faith on the Scriptures and accordingly laid stress on the capacity to read God's Word [7], for as Locke had said, the Bible and the Bible alone was the religion of Protestants.

The Church however had its own special reasons for being concerned to spread day education as well as those it shared with dissent. Firstly the Church had let lapse what control it had exerted over day education in the eighteenth century. In the early part of the eighteenth century some charity schools in Lancashire were in touch with the S.P.C.K. in London and this connection gave them some formal Anglican status since only Anglican literature was supposed to be used for teaching. There were twenty-one such schools in the county in union in 1750 [8]. But direct contact with the S.P.C.K. largely ceased after the 1750s and it is very dubious indeed how far such schools could still be regarded as formally Anglican by the end of the century [9]. The other formal means of Church control had been through the episcopal licensing of schoolmasters, but this practice also had declined into insignificance. For example for four important deaneries covering a wide area of south Lancashire, licensing declined from 14 in 1783 down to 2 in 1804 [10]. The creation of the National Society was thus necessary for the reassertion of Anglican influence in day education which by the turn of the century was virtually a dead letter. The Church felt the need to regain this control in the early decades of the nineteenth century for a mixture of both national and local reasons. Nationally the Church of England faced challenges from several quarters. The Catholics were emancipated and the first Catholic chapel since the Reformation was consecrated in 1835, the bishops were defeated over the Reform Bill, municipal reform in 1835 clarified the absolute right of dissenters to hold public office, there were rows about Church rates and the Ecclesiastical Commission was established to reform the finances of the Church. Accordingly, as Professor Chadwick has noted, 'English Churchmen felt themselves under assault', and William IV died in 1837 muttering his unease about the Church [11].

Within Lancashire this unease was intensely felt. The local clergy were goaded by fears that if facilities were not provided for the new communities then they would fall a prey to dissent. One Lancashire clergyman wrote to the National Society in terms of beleaguered belligerence, 'Flaxmoss is a stronghold of dissent on which I am anxious to make a vigorous attack. What I want is a school . . .' [12]. Such apprehensions were especially keen in the north-east of the county where nonconformity thrived among remote, backward and often turbulent communities. What was worse, religious dissent in Lancashire was often regarded as being linked with political disaffection and the term 'political and religious dissent' was often used to bracket the two. Thus Church education could have political motives in saving children from the 'political excess' and 'bad political influence' that prompted Marsden and Preston clergy to schoolbuilding. At Rawtenstall too the clergyman was appalled to find that the Methodists had become so imbued with what he called Manchester 'liberalism' that they had turned their chapel into a reading room, newsroom, and lecture hall, 'a complete omnibus' he noted with disparagement [13]. In the 1830s with mass and often rowdy protest movements like Chartism and those over factory and poor-law reform afoot in the county the Church was concerned with day schools for their secondary role in inducing civilized behaviour in a population whose resentments could easily get out of hand. Having seen something of the motives of the Societies we may now turn to consider the conflict between them and the reasons for Anglican supremacy dealing with the areas of organization, finance, growth, teacher supply and method, and inspection and visitation.

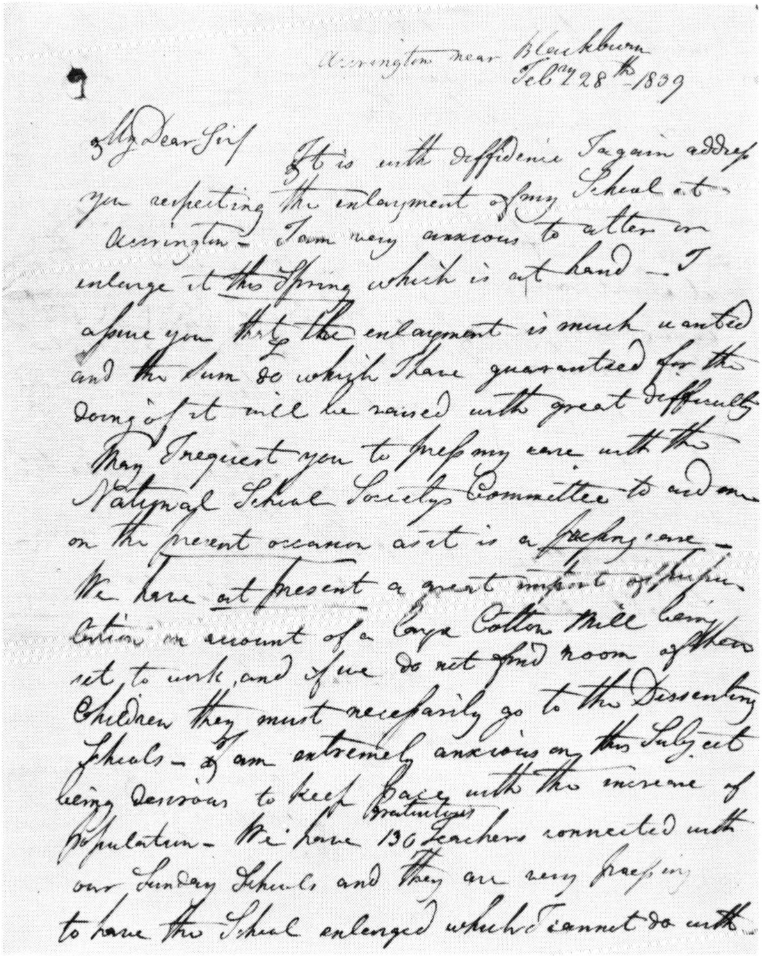

Fig. 1. Letter from Rev. J. Hopwood to National Society, 28 February 1839.
(N.S.L.F. Accrington.)

II

The first area in which we may contrast the strengths of the two societies in Lancashire is in the efficiency of their organization. The heart of the matter was that whereas the National Society had an excellent administrative structure, the British Society had scarcely any.

The National Society arose from the work and ideas of the Rev.

Andrew Bell who had been active in Church education in India. Bell, writing of his experiences in 1811, was then drawn into controversy with Joseph Lancaster who had already published an account of his similar teaching methods in London a few years earlier. In 1811 a committee under the Archbishop of Canterbury met on the S.P.C.K. premises in London to begin this new National Society on the lines proposed by Bell and devoted to specifically Anglican day education [14]. Its purpose was to provide grants of money to help local clergymen to build schoolhouses, to provide teachers using Bell's methods and strictly Anglican literature from the S.P.C.K.

Lancashire was in touch with this movement from the beginning since the Bishop of Chester, under whose jurisdiction the county fell, was present at the initial meeting. Accordingly when it was decided by the Society that the best way of carrying out their objects was to form organizations at diocesan and district level, Chester was one of the first to form in 1812 [15]. This covered the whole of the county and within Lancashire itself Blackburn [16] and Manchester formed local district societies, the Manchester [17] Society alone linking up thirteen schools in and around the city [18]. Many of these would not of course be new schools but already established institutions willing to accept the Society's conditions. Bishop Law of Chester was naturally eager for schools to join and prepared a circular to this effect [19].

In the 1820s, although the Society extended its influence in the county there was little of importance in organizational changes. In 1830, however, a Preston clergyman suggested to London that Lancashire be divided into smaller districts for closer control [20]. Since the first two or three years of the Society there had been district committees only in Blackburn and Manchester, but with the approval of this suggestion in 1832 twelve more local societies were set up in other centres – Burnley, Rochdale, Bury and so forth, to be concerned not only with their own towns but with the area around [21]. The Blackburn Committee which was the first and the only one with ample surviving documentation provides some example of their activities. It was formed in 1812 partly at the instigation of the local Friends of the Sunday Schools who wanted some co-ordinating organization to raise funds to counter the dissenters [22]. The activities of the district committee were dull but highly efficient. Under their chairman the Rev. Dr Whittaker they collected annual attendance figures to keep schools up to the mark, decided where it was most fitting to open schools in relation to suburban population growths, divided the town into areas for collecting money and urging children to attend school [23]. Having one central secretary also relieved some of the work of the London office, and local school secretaries could write to the immensely able and energetic Dr Whittaker about their own trivialities while Whittaker acted as a linch pin between the schools and the secretary in London [24].

In 1839 with the raising of the government grant for education, first introduced in 1833, and the formation of the Committee of Privy Council to administer it, the National Society considered that at the local level it needed an even tighter form of organization to enable it to take the fullest advantage of the new financial opportunities. Thus a movement developed to create a Diocesan Board of Education covering Lancashire, to bring into being, in fact, the abortive idea first mooted in 1812.

In January 1839 a meeting was held at Chester and the Diocesan Board formed itself with the Hon. and Rev. Horace Powys, the energetic Rector of Warrington, as secretary [25]. The purpose was to set up beneath the Board local boards and to link these with the committees of existent National Schools. Publicity was essential and this was the function of a great meeting at Warrington gathering leading Anglican personalities of the county and what Powys termed the 'influential folk' [26]. The resolutions of the meeting crystallized the purpose of the organization – to provide a training college at Chester, to have a diocesan inspector, a subscription fund and deanery committees [27]. Throughout the spring the deaneries – Amounderness, Furness, Manchester, Warrington, Blackburn – set up their own boards and their own district committees [28] and a host of publicity meetings were held throughout the county to reaffirm the links between Church, State and education [29]. By September the structure was completed and the first report published by the new diocesan committee in Chester [30].

It will be evident that the National Society and the Church were profoundly conscious of the importance of creating structures of authority and responsibility for initiative at the local level, without which any pretended 'national' movement would have been a hollow sham. The importance of this is even clearer when we compare the deficiencies of the British Society in this regard.

In its origins the British Society was even earlier in the field than the National. It evolved as an organization through a series of committees formed to manage the affairs of Joseph Lancaster. As a private schoolmaster in St George's Fields in 1798 Lancaster had worked out his method of using older pupils to teach the younger and from 1805 the school attracted fashionable attention when Lancaster was received by George III who subscribed £1,000 [31]. It was at this meeting that Lancaster determined to expand his activities beyond London and thus his project became relevant to Lancashire. From 1806 he made successive tours, visiting Liverpool in that year and yet again in 1808 [32] and 1809 when he visited Manchester also [33]. In Manchester he made friends with the influential dissenters and commercial men Benjamin Braidley [34] and Isaac Crewdson and his plan was tried out before it was finally agreed to build a Lancasterian School in honour of George III's jubilee which was opened in 1813 [35].

The other early school in the county was that in Lancaster. In 1809 William Wilberforce agreed to support the project [36] run by Mrs Ford, the wife of the squire of Ellel Hall, and after an unsatisfactory start it became an increasing success, catering for 240 boys [37]. This case incidentally illustrates that in the early days of the Lancasterian Society it was genuinely non-denominational; after 1811 however it would have been less likely for such a school to receive the support of an Anglican such as Wilberforce. In 1810 Joseph Lancaster toured further but his affairs having deteriorated the Finance Committee was formed which eventually became the British and Foreign Schools Society in 1814. And yet the éclat of the circumstances of some of Lancaster's school openings and the celebrity of some of the people whose support he could elicit does not disguise the fact that the formation of schools under this Society was all too *ad hoc*. There was no organizational structure in the county or at any lower level within the British Society; rather it was merely a question of individual schools choosing, often erratically, to write to London giving a brief report. In these circumstances there was little that the Society could do to extend its activities and it scarcely knew from one year to the next how many Lancasterian schools there were. Indeed it was not even clear what, if anything, constituted a Lancasterian school. In the Anglican case on the other hand it was quite clear; being in union with the National Society entailed receiving visitation and the authority of the bishop. Being a Lancasterian school entailed no such comparable obligations. The reports of the Society contain recurrent complaints of the lack of contact between London and the provinces and they assumed that many schools must be adopting Lancasterian methods without being in touch with the Society. The 1829 Report suggested the formation of county associations of British schools but apart from Buckinghamshire

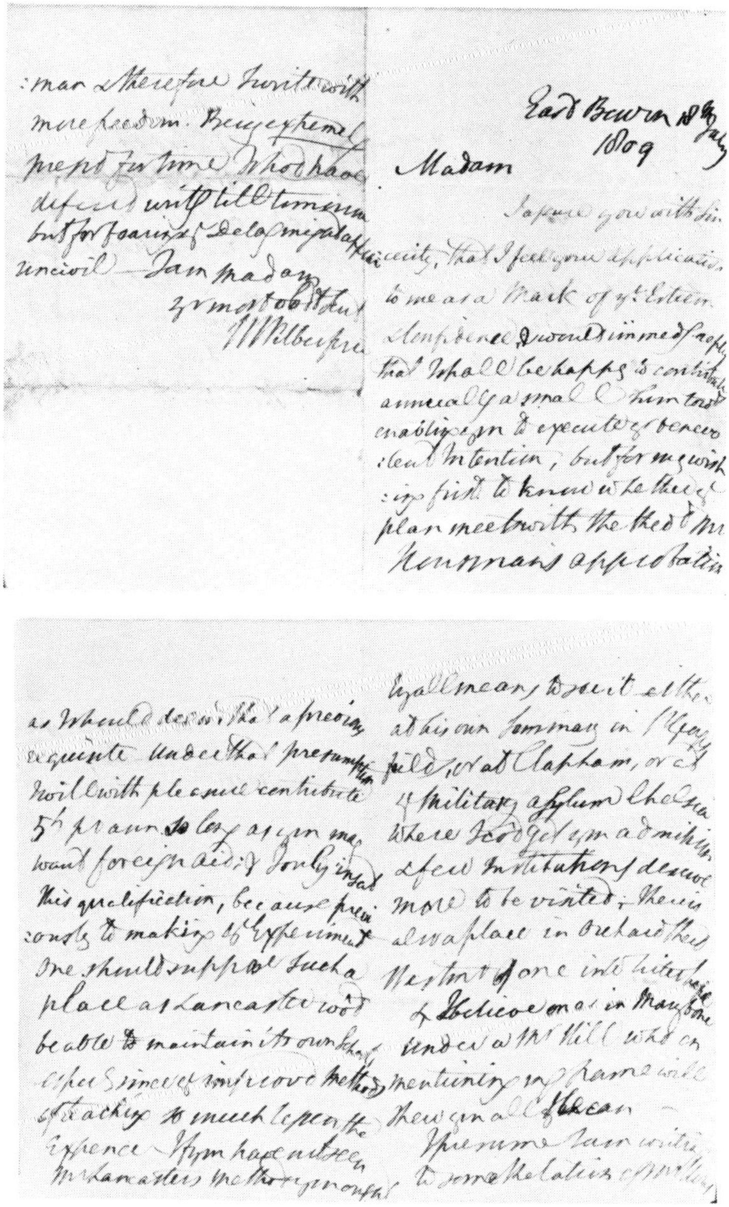

East Bourn 18th July 1809

Madam

I assure you with sincerity, that I feel your application to me as a Mark of yr Esteem & Confidence, & would immedly reply that I shall be happy to contribute annually a small sum towd enabling you to execute yr benevolent Intention, but for my wishing first to know whether yr plan meet with the Revd Mr Housman's approbation as I should deem that a previous requisite. Under that presumption I will with pleasure contribute 5£ p ann so long as you may want foreign aid, & I only insert this qualification, because previously to making the Experiment One should suppose such a place as Lancaster wd be able to maintain its own School espec. since the improved method of teaching so much lessens the Expence. If you have not seen Mr Lancaster's method you ought by all means to visit either at his own Seminary in St George's fields, or at Clapham, or at ye Military asylum Chelsea, where I could get you admission. A few Institutions deserve more to be visited & there is also a place in Orchard Street Westmr & one in Little ... in Marybone under a Mr Hill who on mentioning my name will shew you all he can.

I presume I am writing to some Relation of Mr Hous:man & therefore I write with more freedom. Being extremely pressed for time I should have deferred writing till tomorrow but for fear of Delay making me appear uncivil. I am Madam

yr most obedt Servt

W Wilberforce

Fig. 2. Letter from William Wilberforce to a lady in Lancaster, 18 July 1809. (Archives of the British and Foreign School Society, Borough Road College.)

there seems no evidence that this was ever done. At the end of the 1830s Henry Dunn, the Secretary of the Society, admitted that he had no means of knowing how many British schools there were and explained why this was so — 'partly on account of the expense, but also, and perhaps chiefly from the fact, that we have no benefits to offer to local schools; we have no ecclesiastical organization and of course there is no motive strong enough to induce parts of the country to correspond regularly with us . . . ' [38]. Thus it was, for example, that there was a school in Blackburn begun in 1810 which called itself 'British' but which never had contact with London [39]. There must have been others half adopting some monitorial system, but whether they were 'Lancasterian' or not is merely a play with words.

The strength of the National Society and the plight of the British reflected the different forms of ecclesiastical organization to which they related. The Church had a natural tradition of organization of the parish, deanery and diocese which nonconformity lacked. Dissent organized too late. The Unitarians in the 1820s, Presbyterians, Congregationalists and Baptists in the 1830s all formed national or regional bodies but even the Methodists who were already organized for general purposes did not set up their committee for education until the 1830s. Consequently over much of this period there was simply no framework within which nonconformist chapels could join to propagate views or co-ordinate a policy of money-raising. It was, for example, impossible to tell how many 'Baptist' chapels there were in Lancashire in 1800 partly because individual congregations and ministers of many sects shifted around in varying degrees of Trinitarianism, Arianism, Arminianism, Calvinism, Antinomianism, Connexionalism and Congregationalism that were the basic ingredients of dissenting faiths. If even the denominations themselves were still in a highly fluid, embryonic and disorganized state at this time, how much more difficult was it to obtain any concerted action among nonconformity as a whole. By striking contrast the early nineteenth-century churchman had merely to refer to Rivington's Clerical Directory to find his co-religionists.

In turn the quality and nature of leadership differed markedly between Church and dissent. In the National Society in the county authority was wielded by the Bishop of Chester. The occupants of this see in the 1820s and 1830s, C.J. Blomfield and J.B. Sumner, were persons of very high ability on their way to higher positions, Blomfield to London and Sumner to the archbishopric of Canterbury. It was indeed fortuitous that the see of Chester being somewhat modest did act as a stepping-stone for relatively young bishops of exceptional ability and Lancashire benefited accordingly. Both Blomfield and Sumner regularly attended meetings of the National Society in London and Sumner in particular was often able to exert a profound influence on policy in the relations between the Society in Lancashire and London. For example all application for Government money for schools sent in by clergymen in Lancashire passed through the bishop's hands. This was no formality as Sumner had a minute knowledge of the county and was able to add comments on local conditions to help the progress of applications. He also played a crucial role in 1839 when the issue of State inspection was raised and many Lancashire parishes wished to reject school-building money rather than submit to it [40]. Sumner kept his head, received assurances that there would be no interference with religion and by persuading the parishes to take the money prevented a severe setback to educational expansion in the county. He was also noted for his rather tolerant statesman-like attitude to Catholics, a traditionally important element in the county whom, unlike some of his clergy, he saw no point in antagonizing. Finally the bishops used their episcopal charges for exhortation and propaganda about education and Sumner laid great stress upon it [41]. Beneath the bishops the Church and the National Society enjoyed the services of highly able, well connected and academically outstanding clergy such as Whittaker at Blackburn and Powys at Warrington on whom much of the brunt of local educational administration fell and who in the 1830s devoted most of their attention to it. In Manchester and Liverpool were others like the Rev. Hugh Stowell and the Rev. H. M'Neile for whom Anglican education amounted almost to an obsession and whose activities have been closely charted elsewhere [42]. Lancashire nonconformity could scarcely match this quality of administrative leadership nor this intensity of interest. There were indeed some notable nonconformist leaders in Lancashire at the time [43], Jabez Bunting the 'Pope' of Methodism, William Roby the Independent, Joseph Harbottle the Baptist, and yet it is no disparagement to say that none of them had quite the ability of Sumner, one of the most distinguished primates of Victorian England. It would be even more true to say that for none of them was education and the British Society a leading or even prominent concern of their activities. Indeed Bunting was well known for his policy of actually cutting back education in Sunday schools. Both in structure and in leadership the National Society began with a very powerful advantage over its rival.

III

Closely related to the different efficiencies of their organizational structures was the second area in which we wish to compare the two societies, namely their financial links with education at the county level. The financial links were of two sorts. First, money was raised in the county by the local branches of the Societies and sent to their London offices, and, second, money was redistributed by their London offices and sent back into the provinces. In these various flows the National Society in Lancashire benefited vastly more than did the British Society, and this further reinforced the former's strength and predominance.

The National Society in London raised subscriptions throughout the country. But in fact very little indeed came from Lancashire and this was largely contributed by the clergy. Apart from Nathaniel Gould who was one of Bell's close friends in the county, the central organization of the National Society scarcely tapped the new commercial wealth of Lancashire, and it was a persistent feature of these years that Lancashire absorbed vast amounts of charitable money from the rest of the country and sent very little beyond its boundaries. At the end of the period Lancashire had taken 13 per cent of all the National Society's grants to the whole of the country but contributed only 8 per cent of the total of the Queen's Letter Fund of 1839 [44]. The National Society derived its wealth largely from London and the south of England *beau monde* and from institutions like the Cambridge colleges. Its importance lay in then transferring this wealth to the needy manufacturing districts. The grants made by the National Society to places in Lancashire rose cumulatively as follows [45]:

Table 1

	£		£
1817	100	1828	2,655
1818	325	1829	3,579
1819	475	1830	4,580
1824	675	1831	5,520
1825	1,025	1832	7,410
1826	1,245	1833	8,735
1827	2,055		

In 1833 came the first State capital grants of £20,000 a year made by the Treasury for school building. Applicants were expected to raise at least half the estimated building cost before applying to the Treasury to make up the rest. Now the Society took on a new function, it was not only a source of funds but an extra channel from a yet wealthier reservoir, for the public money before 1839 could be obtained only through one of the religious societies. Lancashire thus gained two forms of financial aid from the Society for the rest of the 1830s as follows:

Table 2

Grants to Lancashire schools from the National Society		Grants to Lancashire schools from the Treasury and secured through the National Society [46]	
	£		£
1834	1,180	1833-8	17,313
1835	347		
1836	555		
1837	1,235		
1838	1,080		

By the end of the period the Society had given to Lancashire nearly £14,000 of its own money and secured from the Treasury over £17,000. It is important to appreciate the importance of the last figure. The National Society secured about 70 per cent of all the Treasury money available between 1833 and 1839 for the country as a whole. Of that Treasury money secured by the National Society Lancashire received 21.5 per cent. This was very much greater than that received by any other area. Even the whole of Yorkshire received less than half what Lancashire received from the Treasury grant through the Society and all other counties were negligible by comparison. It was quite evident that the National Society was throwing the disproportionate bulk of its resources into Lancashire which in turn was quite the most active in applying for grants. This willingness to accord a quite exceptional and special place to Lancashire was yet another strength in the Society's strategy in the county.

The British Society's financial links with Lancashire, like its organizational links, were much weaker. Local societies in the county were supposed to raise money to send to London. However it cannot be said that Lancashire viewed this aspect of the connection with other than profound apathy. To take a few examples, in 1809 they sent £60 out of a national total of £454 – a peculiarly large amount that was not repeated – then in 1810 £10 out of £1,537, in 1811 nothing out of £2,141 and in 1812 5 guineas out of £2,036. These were sums almost derisory in their smallness. Regular contributors were very few, John Ford of Ellel among the gentry and Cropper, Benson and Co. and Rathbone, Hodgson and Co. in trade. This was consistent with the normal pattern of philanthropy: Lancashire had so many problems internally that it did not send large sums outside the county. In the 1830s when the county began to receive Government money through the British Society so the sending of money by county auxiliaries to London did revive and in 1835 ten auxiliary committees in Lancashire sent a total of £204 to the British Society in London.

But with the British Society the reverse side of the coin seems to be missing. Whereas the National Society sent very considerable sums into Lancashire there is no trace that the British Society performed the same function for Lancashire British schools before 1833. It may well have been the sharp realization that no London money was forthcoming that caused this drastic collapse of sending money from Lancashire to London between 1809 and 1811. The 1818 Report of the Society stated clearly that it did not give financial assistance. The 1825 Report stated that due to their limited funds they could give only 'a very feeble and partial co-operation'. In 1829 they very vaguely and cagily suggested that they would act to communicate between wealthy auxiliaries and poor and distressed districts, implying that money would change hands. But generally before 1833 any money coming into Lancashire from the British Society – and we have no trace of any – if it existed at all must have been quite negligible. In the cases where we have documentation for local British schools in the county there is no trace of any receipt of money from the British Society in London [47]. In any case the British Society itself was in chronic debt. Between 1821 and 1839 it was in debt for nine years·and had a balance for seven, but four of the seven balances were less than £45 and seven of the nine deficits were over £300. Even the Royal Lancasterian School in Manchester, one of the earliest and one with most detailed financial evidence, was in chronic debt in this period. It seemed simply to be a fact, which some Lancashire sources were not slow to point out, that education was not high in nonconformist priorities when it came to disbursing funds. The *Blackburn Mail* for example pointed out in 1827 that whereas the Methodists alone had raised £45,000 for foreign missions yet the nonconformists altogether could muster only £9,000 for the British Society [48].

The 1833 Government grant had a stimulating effect on the British Society just as it had on its rival as we may see from the grants secured in Table 2. But while the grant did enable the Society to begin contributions to school provision in the county the endeavour as a whole was still of a very disappointing nature. Whereas up to 1838 the British Society had secured £2,314 for twelve places in Lancashire, the National Society had secured over £17,000. Secondly within the Society itself the Lancashire effort was not proportional to the significance of the county. From 1834 to 1837 fourteen applications were officially listed from Lancashire, but Yorkshire had eighteen more and Devon and Cornwall each almost as many. While Lancashire was disproportionately important in National Society activity, it was disproportionately unimportant in that of the British Society.

These strictures relate to the financial relations between the British Society in London, the Treasury and the county. Within Lancashire itself some elements of British Society finance were on a better footing and the grounds of criticism are different. Within large cities the British Society fared quite well, and even better than the National Society in some respects. For example in Manchester it is possible to examine the proportions of key business occupations supporting the National and British Societies of the city around 1830 [49].

Table 3 *Percentage of select Manchester occupations supporting the Manchester bodies of the National and British Societies, c. 1830.*

	cotton spinners	cotton merchants	cotton manufacturers
National Society	4.2	nil	12.9
British Society	16.8	11.9	22.8

The manufacturers in both cases clearly felt a stronger commitment to the local labour force and its education than the merchants who, in any case, employed fewer workpeople. Within Lancashire the British Society was able to benefit from the support of a number of prominent nonconformist men of business, Benjamin Heywood and Isaac Crewdson, Manchester bankers, Mark Philips of Stand, John Bright and Richard Cobden, James Thomson the distinguished calico printer of

Clitheroe, and the Liverpool circle of James Cropper, Robert Benson, the Rathbones, George Holt and Samuel Hope. An analysis of the sponsorship of the Bolton British School also amply displays the commercial nature of this support [50]. But although the British Society was able to tap the wealth of the industrial and commercial elites in the large cities for projects within those cities, this meant that the Society had a few good schools — Circus Street, Duncan Street, Mosley Street, for example — in Manchester and Liverpool but few elsewhere. The British Society in Lancashire was essentially a limited urban movement. It made little headway in agricultural districts like West Derby, none at all in Amounderness and Lonsdale, while Furness seemed to be virtually abandoned in spite of an indigenous Baptist and Quaker tradition. Perhaps more surprising was the failure to make headway in the valley of Burnley or over the hills south into Rossendale where the Church felt itself threatened by dissent.

The National Society by contrast was a more genuinely county-wide movement for the obvious reason that as well as being able to tap businessmen in cities — though in Manchester to a lesser degree than dissent — it also commanded the support of the gentry in the country-side, most of whom were Anglican. This was of profound significance since local Anglican landowners frequently gave sites for schools outright from their own land and played a more crucial role in educational movements in the countryside than any individual businessman could do in a city. Lord Derby, the Duke of Hamilton, Lord Skelmersdale, Sir Henry Hoghton, Squire Clifton, the Gibsons of Quernmoor, Lady Cavendish of Holker, the Leghs of Lyme, the Butlers of Kirkland, Sir Thomas Hesketh of Rufford, R. Townley Parker, the Earl of Witton, Sir Oswald Mosley, Sir Joseph Radcliffe, Le Gendre Starkie, Lord Suffield and Earl Howe were all Anglican gentry with interests in Lancashire giving land and supporting the National Society chiefly in the rural areas of the county. There was simply no comparable large class of nonconformist gentry on whom the British Society could call, since those who were not Anglican were Catholic and accordingly not usually interested in, if not hostile to, either society. Nonconformity in the countryside and without the resources of its commercial elite in the cities was financially poor, and the national organization of the British Society did little to redress that poverty. Weak organization begat weak finance and this in turn begat weak growth, to which we should now turn.

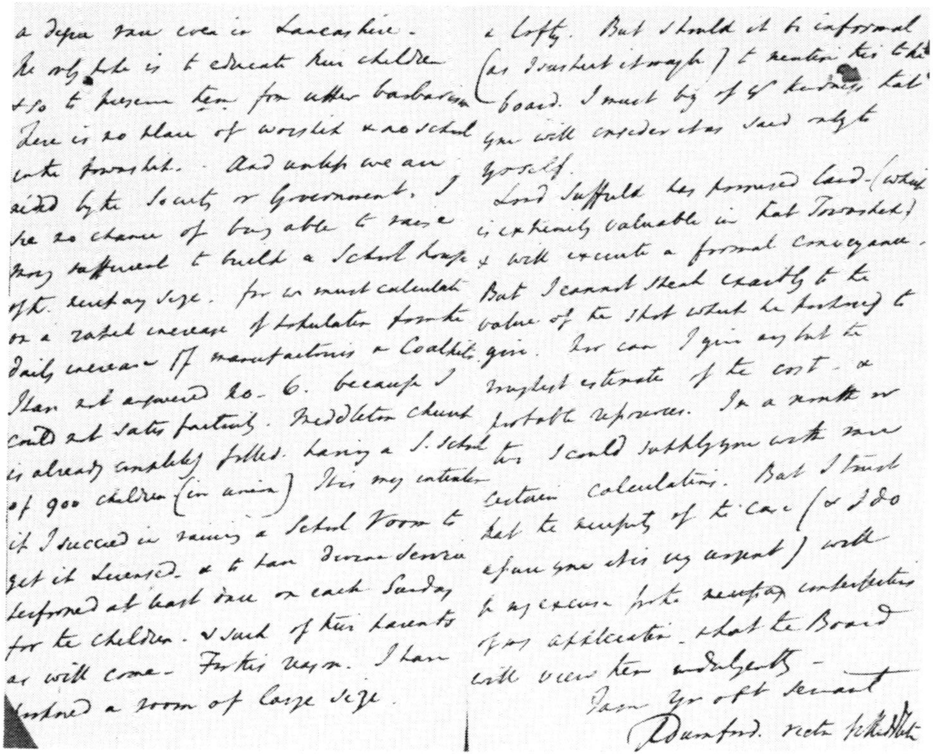

Fig. 3. Letter from Rev. R. Durnford to National Society, 7 October 1835. (N.S.L.F. Thornham.)

IV

It is scarcely surprising that since the National Society had shown itself to be so much more effective in organization and finance than its rival, so too its growth in the county was superior to that of the British Society. The expansion of the National Schools in Lancashire was considerable. Although the figures should not be taken too exactly as some schools ceased to report, there was always confusion concerning whether a school was directly or indirectly linked and so forth, some idea of the numbers may be gained from the available figures below:

Table 4 *Lancashire day schools in union with the National Society*

1814	2
1815	11
1816	26
1817	37
1818	38
1820	49
1827	76
1830	110
1832	139
1835	222
1838	239 (16,500 boy
	12,987 girl
	day scholars)

These were calculated from the lists in the annual reports. We are sceptical about the sequence of the last three numbers; there is no doubt that there was this great rise during the period of the State grant and we have discovered 102 manuscript files for new places between 1833 and 1839, but they are spread through the years, there is no sudden rise between 1832 and 1835. However, the number of files suggests that the size of the increase is about right. On the other hand, that a local committee came into union in this period does not mean to say that it had a school which was a going concern since there would be a time lag before it was built. But at any rate the numbers of places with schools or erecting them is impressive.

Another check from another source on the number of National Schools in the county is provided by Horace Powys's survey for the setting-up of the Diocesan Board in 1839 [51].

Table 5 *Parochial schools in the Lancashire deaneries 1839*

Deanery	Total schools	In union with the National Society	National system adopted wholly or in part
Amounderness	139	24	62
Blackburn	113	66	80
Copeland and Kendal	115	9	47
Furness	70	9	18
Manchester	167	49	73
Warrington	176	40	105
	780	197	385

The old endowed schools evidently still continued uncommitted to any particular religious form and they still exceeded those schools actually in union with the Society. Powys's figures obviously differ slightly from those of the National Society itself; the latter thought there were just over 200 schools in union, Powys just under, but it gives some idea of the total so far as it is knowable.

If we turn to the growth of the British Society in the county we find in Table 6 twelve schools having some connection with the Society between 1809 and 1833. The smallness of this compared with the 139 in union with the National Society in 1832 is evident. That the 1833 grant proved a stimulus to the British Society is also clear from Table 7, twenty schools making applications for grants and fifteen being awarded them between 1834 and 1839. But again this was very small compared with the achievement of the National Society. This was also reflected in the differences of numbers of children taught. The National Society claimed to have 16,500 boys and 12,987 girl day pupils in the county at the end of the 1830s, a total of 29,487. If we add the places provided by new British school building under the Treasury grant to the latest figures of the pre-existing British schools we arrive at a total of 9,703. Even if we add on a notional 2,400 to account for the eight schools where we have no totals and according them a generous putative total of 300 each our grand total would still only come to 12,103, considerably less than half of the capacity of the National Schools.

Table 6 *The structure of the British and foreign school society in Lancashire 1809-33*

Place	Date																									
	1800 9 10 11 12 13 14 15 16 17 18 19 20 21 22 23 24 25 26 27 28 29 30 31 32 33

Liverpool

Liverpool Duncan St.   206 boys   196 boys

225 girls   125 girls

Liverpool Irish School   400 children

Liverpool Circus St.

Manchester   923 children   997 children   1020 children

Warrington   ?

Lancaster

Bolton   60 children

Great Harwood   40 children

Downham   70 boys

Rochdale   75 girls

Bury

Blackburn   100 children? Probably typical of private schools calling themselves 'British'.

The lines on the diagram indicate that there is evidence of the existence of a British school for the dates and places shown. Where possible, boys' and girls' attendance are marked respectively above and below the line of each particular school. Where these are not distinguished the total number of children is marked above the line. Short broken lines indicate that the evidence is fragmentary, question marks that the schools' existence or duration is doubtful.

Table 7 *Treasury grants to British Schools in Lancashire 1834-9*

		1834	1835	1836	1837	1838	1839
Oldham	2032	G254					
Blackburn Nova Scotia	300	A	G150	Cong.			
Blackburn East	300		G150				
Over Darwen	125	A	G125	Bapt.			
Lancaster	300	A	G150				
Manchester	840	A			G420		
Charleston	150	A	G 75	A	Cong.		
Bolton	1000		A	G500	Quaker		
Southport	120		A	G 60	Cong.		
Cockerbrook	100		A		G169	Bapt.	
Salford	400		A		G300	A	Cong.
Liverpool	?		A				
Toxteth Park	?		A				
Churchtown	?			A	Cong.		
Chorlton	?			A	∧		
Preston	1000					A	G500
Milnrow	180					A	G 90
Salford	500					A	G 50
Warrington	?						A
Rochdale	500			A	G250		

7847 pupils

A stands for the year of application and G for the year of the grant. In the diagram the first column of figures represents the number of day places provided by the new school, where known. The numbers following G are the amount of Treasury grant in £. Where the leading sponsors are known we add a suggestion of the sect that seems especially to be supporting the application, eg Cong. = Congregationalist, Bapt. = Baptist. The Treasury files of applications on which the table is based are in the archives of the Department of Education and Science.

This disparity of growth both in school formation and capacity is the inevitable result of the disparity in organizational and financial performance we have been examining so far.

V

When the schools were built and operating the two societies could offer two further services to them, the supply of teachers and inspection and visitation. Both societies took teacher-training seriously. The National Society started a central school at Baldwin's Gardens where it remained until its transfer to Westminster in 1832. But a few weeks after this decision the hope was expressed that the Diocesan and District Committees would gradually attend to their own needs 'and train up teachers' [52]. Thus from the outset there were to be two sources of supply, the central and the local, but the effective level of the latter in Lancashire proved to be not the diocese but the larger towns.

The long-standing links of Lancashire schools with the School Committee and training school in London may be seen in the following way [53].

Teachers sent from London to

1814	Manchester, Walton-le-Dale, Preston
1816	Bolton, Lancaster
1817	Everton and Kirkdale
1818	Bury
1825	Preston
1827	Wigan, Whitewell
1828	Stand
1833	Preston
1834	Preston
1836	Preston
1837	Preston, Ormskirk (2), Warrington
1838	Rochdale, Liverpool

Between the period of first demand up to 1818 and that of the Government grant of 1833, there was a marked decline in the central school's function as a supplier to Lancashire. But here the local centres came into play.

The original intention was that Chester should be developed as a training centre for the diocese. Certainly activity was considerable in the formation of the first diocesan society in 1812. It was founded in January, and in March the parent society was asked for a master 'as we are in hopes of having a central school here in the course of a few weeks' [54]. This burst of activity produced some results and thirty-two masters were trained for teaching in the diocese, but there were signs of its limitation, for very few Lancashire benefactors supported it. As the report candidly noted, 'some members who have established schools in their own immediate neighbourhoods have withdrawn their subscriptions to the diocesan school' [55]. Next year it was asserted that it was closely following improvements at Baldwin's Gardens, but there was no indication of sending teachers to Lancashire [56]. In 1821 Lancaster did send a master there for training [57], but a gradual change in relationships was emerging as we can see in the national annual reports. In 1815 it was assumed that Manchester had hived off from the diocesan society, by 1818 the Chester school was listed merely as the school of the Chester deanery, by 1830 it was noted that 'a diocesan society formerly existed . . .' [58]. The correspondence ceased in 1817, no reports were sent after 1818 and it was clear that the second diocesan movement of 1839 had to recreate the whole structure afresh [59].

Apart from London, the Barrington school at Bishop Auckland was the leading external source for the county. This was started in 1810 by the Bishop of Durham, and by 1813 a monitor from there had been touring and organizing schools in Lancashire, Manchester being one of his centres [60]. Accrington applied there for a master [61], and Bell himself sent the Lancaster master there — and not to London — to learn the latest improvements [62]. It was Liverpool, however, that became the chief training centre in the county, and in view of Bell's constant visits there, this was probably his deliberate intention. Lancaster asked it to take six boys for training in 1815 [63], they applied for a master there in 1827 [64], and sent a mistress shortly afterwards [65]. As early as 1816 it was being used for Cheshire, even in preference to the diocesan school [66], and in 1831 the superintendent wrote 'there are besides eleven masters and mistresses present with us two of whom are for the Catholic schools in the town; and we have before had either five or seven of their teachers', and he observed that the master of St Andrews regarded Liverpool as superior to the London central school and Edinburgh as a training institution [67]. When Liverpool itself applied to London for a teacher it was only for a 'very superior' one at the unusual salary of £120 or more [68]. But the devolution went yet further. In 1819, Lancaster was acting as a centre for retraining existing masters in surrounding parishes [69], and Lady Cavendish of Holker sent two for training in 1827 [70]. Burnley [71], Preston and of course Manchester [72] also served as training schools. Notwithstanding this, the Rev. Horace Powys, ever eager for new fields of activity, suggested that his own school at Warrington should become a central school [73] and secured a superintendent for this new department [74]. The National Society had thus created a very ample provision for teacher training both outside and within the county for its growing schools.

The British Society likewise not only engaged in teacher-training but had set up at Borough Road the very first of the training colleges, with records of men teachers from 1804. From 1811 however began the significant phase with the formation of the Finance Committee reflected in a rapid increase in the number of intakes. At this stage, one John Lovell came to Borough Road from Colne but passed on after training to Bedfordshire. In 1819 William Evans was sent to Liverpool after ten months training and in July 1820 James Crossley to Lancaster after four months [75]. The relevance of the Borough Road training school to the county was therefore only slight. Of the 206 men trained only these two went to Lancashire — indeed less than half the number it trained for St Petersburg. The same was so with women's teacher training [76]. In 1819 Susannah Williams of London went to Swansea and was then reappointed to Liverpool. The only other case was that of Sarah Glover, also from London, who went to Lime Street School, Liverpool, in 1826. Again these were only two out of a total of 216 women, the same number went to Buenos Aires.

Here again, even in an area like teacher-training in which they were specially active, the British Society fell behind the National. The National focused its activities sharply within Britain to provide teachers for its schools. The British with far more slender resources took on the more glamorous role of trying to supply teachers to half the world with the consequence that Lancashire received only a minute fraction of its output. As in so much else the British Society almost seemed to have withdrawn from a vigorous contest with its Anglican rival in this most important English theatre of their confrontation.

As regards the content of teaching and teaching method there was probably little to choose between the Societies. As is well known the characteristic feature of the teaching method of both Societies was the use of monitors to cope with very large numbers by teaching small parts of lessons [77]. The argument between Bell and Lancaster as to whose was the prior or superior system reached fantastic degrees of triviality. Bell was accused of copying the use of slates [78], Lancaster of copying Bell's use of sand, Bell had no desks but only forms, Lancaster, it was claimed, had desks for all [79]. But in practice, at the local level schools seemed to work out their own modifications which probably made the differences between the systems slight, apart from the crucial one of the teaching of Anglican doctrine.

Warrington National School, for example, made modifications which it admitted brought it more into line with British practice although it was a National School. They had desks for a third of the room and galleries at either end and what was learned in the class was repeated in the desks [80]. Again the National School at Ashton-in-Makerfield devised its own way of training the monitors for part of the day [81]. This system of delegating authority and the repetition of lessons in small sections was a useful way of teaching large numbers but it also led to a deadening rote learning. At Wigan the worst effects were apparent: 'our plan is to hear them a portion of Scripture containing from fourteen to twenty or twenty-six verses; this they learn during the month and likewise some questions containing answers and references' [82]. Likewise the Warrington National School was criticised for not inducing 'inquiry into the why and wherefore' but merely rendering children 'the dupes and slaves to a system and a sect' [83]. The British Society did not consider itself superior in this regard. While they praised the work of Pestalozzi and von Fellenberg they admitted that 'our concern is with the million; and here the question is only what is practicable' [84].

But if both were similar in their monitorial and rote teaching systems yet in fairness we should note that in Lancashire the British Schools were pioneers of some imaginative developments in curriculum. This was unusual in being an area in which the balance of evidence suggests a superiority of the British Schools over the National. For example printing was taught at the Circus Street British School in Liverpool [85], at the Bolton British School they taught mechanical engineering especially of steam engines [86] and at Lancaster navigation and arithmetic up to cube roots [87]. The Manchester Lancasterian School also developed the teaching of arithmetic as a particular forte and the master had devised a teaching machine for the multiplication of money and the conversion of units of money [88].

This seems to have had some influence since it was also adopted at the Lancaster school. With the exception of an abortive attempt at tailoring at Warrington [89] we do not find such developments at National Schools at the time, though some older endowed schools often had interesting practical variants in curriculum before the formation of the National Society.

VI

The fourth area where we may compare the performance of the Societies was in that of visitation and inspection at the local level, a vitally important function that prompted new centres to form schools or to become associated with societies and which kept in a state of efficiency those already formed. Here yet again, for another set of reasons, the National Society was pre-eminent.

The National Society even from its earliest days used a variety of agents to spread the system and these inevitably found their way to Lancashire. At least from 1813 a Mr Grover was being paid two guineas a week to organize and visit schools. In this year he arranged a school near Bolton and reported back on it [90]. In July in the same year he formed a school at Moss Bank and then moved to Manchester [91]. In 1814 he was advising the trustees of Bury School [92] and then passes out of the picture as an agent sent to Rochdale in 1815 [93]. The next agent was the Rev. R.W. Bamford. In 1814 he was being ordered by the School Committee to go to Manchester and Liverpool [94]. The next year he was in Preston [95] and was there yet again in the following year [96], whence he moved to Liverpool. In 1817 he resigned and stayed in Liverpool permanently as the superintendent of the Bluecoat School.

Bamford worked, or was supposed to work, in conjunction with Dr Bell himself for Bell was not only the fount and expounder of the method but was also the chief visitor to see that it was carried out. In 1812 Bell was staying with his friend Lord Kenyon, a Cheshire landowner who had been present with the Bishop of Chester at the formation of the Society in 1811. He moved to visit Liverpool, where he took measures 'as I believe will suffice to plant the system . . .' [97], and there he found his old Indian acquaintance General Dirom who was himself by coincidence corresponding with the Commander-in-Chief about Madras schools [98]. This had already borne fruit, for shortly afterwards Bell visited Warrington, where a military school for regimental children was being conducted so successfully as to attract in addition as many civilians as it would hold [99]. Thence Bell proceeded to Manchester, to Preston and then to the Lake District to stay with William Wordsworth. In 1813 there were further visits to Manchester and Preston with Kenyon, and contacts with Dirom. But whether Bell was there or not, Lord Kenyon was regularly touring. In 1813 Bell wrote to him, 'nothing can rejoice me more than your Lordship's condescension in visiting the schools. I know no other person whom I can so entirely rely on [100]. In the following year when Bell had been ill, he wondered whether he could catch Kenyon 'before you set out for Lancashire' [101]. Kenyon went alone to Manchester, and his report disturbed Bell – 'I grieve about Manchester' [102] – but Liverpool was in good form and by October Bell rushed there himself. 'The Bluecoat delights me . . . the Ladies' scolded, and greatly improving. The Moorfields' school insufferably bad' [103], and at Everton he was fretting that the school should be united during his stay and complaining of their want of books [104].

There was much of the old womanish fussy busybody in Bell, but his driving, well-intentioned energy was beyond question. In 1815, he was back again in Liverpool, visiting Bolton and Manchester, and staying with his friend the local education supporter Nathaniel Gould [105]. Bamford at this time was supposed to be under Bell's or Kenyon's directions, and in 1815 toured with Bell in Liverpool and Manchester. After this he toured independently to Ulverston, Lancaster, Preston and elsewhere and in spite of Bell's attempts at direction he seems to have pleased himself [106]. Another friend of Bell's, Dr Briggs, accompanied Bell to Preston in 1812, and wrote to him from Liverpool where he lived; he seems also to have done some local visiting, for example to Poulton-le-Fylde [107]. These Lancashire tours of Bell continued in 1816, 1817, 1818, 1820 and 1822. In 1823, unable to appear himself, Bell sent his secretary Mr Davies who sent reports from Liverpool [108]. In 1824 he was there again, setting up schools in Ulverston [109], and also in 1828 [110].

In 1830 Bell began his last illness, but still received letters from Liverpool [111]. The death of Bell left something of a gap, and in 1838 it was proposed to establish a new system of inspection. Something of this was done in Lancashire and we find the Rev. J. Rushton acting as a general superintendent and inspector of poor villages in the north-east. He visited Downham as what he termed 'the inspector of National Schools in our district' [112] and wrote to the London Office for Inspectors' returns referring to 'certain schools which the Bishop of Chester commissions me to inspect' [113]. Clearly having this system of inspection, keeping schools up to standard, ensuring adequate supplies of books and teachers and urging places without schools to start them was yet a further strength to the Society and one in which it far surpassed the British schools.

By contrast British Society visitation and use of agents was much less thorough. Joseph Lancaster for all his faults had provided a link between London and the provinces by his travels and he had focused much of his attention on Lancashire. With his going a serious gap was left. Then in 1817 a first itinerant was sent out to re-establish the links broken by Lancaster's removal and it was reported that 'Miss Springham has visited several schools in the North' [114]. But this was not regular and there was no reference to Lancashire. The negative implications of William Allen's journal are suggestive. He was the Treasurer of the Society and a man of ability who very frequently visited Lancashire for various purposes. And yet only once in the whole of his travels did he trouble to visit a British School in the county [115]. Contrasted with Bell's almost obsessive visiting, prying and persuading it reveals in the Society a difference in outlook and in this as in much else they were far from sufficiently active in keeping links between London and the localities.

At last in 1826 came a genuine move in policy to try to achieve a greater cohesion as Captain Bromley was appointed as the travelling agent. By the beginning of 1827 he was in Rochdale where he spoke at the Flying Horse and was well received [116]. Later in 1831 another agent was appointed, Lieutenant Fabian who formed the Manchester auxiliary society [117]. Here very belatedly – just as their rival Bell was removed from the scene – was a genuine attempt to improve the efficiency of the Society by achieving the same kind of close links between London and the provinces that the National Society already had. Lieutenant Fabian's activity in Lancashire in the 1830s was one of the elements behind the greater vigour of the Society in that decade. As well as forming the Manchester auxiliary he held the public meeting in Preston that began the Society there in 1835 [118]; in 1837 he spoke on education at the Manchester Athenaeum [119] and made contact with Richard Cobden and Henry Ashworth. As an illustration of the workings of local influence and national organization Ashworth's own account could scarcely be bettered.

Mr Cobden and I met in Manchester with Mr Thomas Wyse M.P. for Waterford . . . also with Lieutenant Fabian, the agent of the British and Foreign School Society, who sought to promote a movement for 'National Education' by raising a number of schools in Manchester to be supported by voluntary subscriptions. Several schools were opened as a result of this effort.

These did not survive the depression but

. . . whilst the feeling in favour of education was still strong I got some of the advanced liberals in Bolton to unite for the purpose of establishing a British school there; and at a meeting which was called for the promotion of that object and which was addressed by Mr Cobden, a sufficient subscription was raised to defray the expense of building. [120]

By the end of the 1830s the use of national agents for visitation was probably the one area in which the British Society really matched the National. But even so, Fabian's activities were no substitute for the close episcopal and deanery watch and control over education that the Church with its existent, permanent structure was able to exert. Nonconformity, not having created its own district and county organization even yet, Fabian was operating still in a situation whose amorphousness reduced his effectiveness.

VII

We have tried to show why in the context of Lancashire the Anglican National Society attained such a position of predominance over its nonconformist rival. The National Society developed a wide-ranging and tightly controlled form of organization based on its pre-existent ecclesiastical administration. Dissent had no such structure binding the denominations together and many of the denominations themselves still lacked any internal organization. Lacking this for their general purposes, they did not create a form of organization specifically to deal with education. Nor was their leadership so interested in education as were leading Anglican clerics in the county. The finance of the Anglican society was far better. The London office sent very considerable sums to Lancashire raised from the south of England, even before 1833. The British Society sent none and received scarcely anything in return. Although the British schools in cities and towns tapped industrial wealth, yet because of the religious cast of the gentry they made virtually no headway in rural areas. After 1833 the National Society gained the lion's share of grants and Lancashire gained the lion's share of the National Society's portion. The relative poverty of nonconformity and the inability of their London organization to top up funds raised in the provinces to qualifying levels kept back the number of applications and grant awards. Accordingly the National Society far outstripped the British in growth having probably about six times as many schools and more than twice as many pupils. In teacher supply the National Society arranged a network of training schools within the county as well as drawing on the central school at Baldwin's Gardens. The Borough Road school of the British Society seemed to conceive its role in more global terms and its contribution to the immediate pressing problem of Lancashire was slight. On the other hand, while the teaching methods of the two societies were fairly similar, the British schools did seem more enterprising in developing new directions in curriculum. Finally the National Society had a highly active form of inspection and visitation, chiefly embodied until the 1830s in the person of Bell himself and his minions, while after the removal of Lancaster the British Society lacked any comparable service. With the death of Bell and the arrival of Fabian in the early 1830s the societies were probably more equal in their provision in this sphere. But the root of the matter was that the National Society took Lancashire very seriously indeed and concentrated a great deal of its effort there. The British Society did not and scarcely seemed to accord the county more importance than Devon and Cornwall. Consequently this difference in their attitudes was reflected throughout these various areas of their comparative performance.

What we have been examining is not merely a piece of local history for it tells us something about the predicament of nonconformity in education in the nineteenth century. It has been the traditional and honourable role of nonconformity in English history to act as a check on the established Church and on the State and to proclaim 'civil and religious liberty' and the rights of the 'nonconformist conscience'. As such it has contributed inestimably to the pluralism of English society through the tolerance of variety in modes of belief. It has also contributed through the creation of forms of voluntary association which have both enriched the texture of English social life and, being interposed between the individual and the State, have served as a safeguard of the one against the other. The failure of nonconformity to provide an alternative education was of serious importance for the future, for its disparity *vis-à-vis* the National Society grew even wider as the latter secured 80 per cent of the Government grants for elementary education between 1839 and the mid-century [121]. The realization that they had lost the conflict was an important element driving dissent into a negative hostility to State aid in education, since with the increasing imbalance of voluntary provision between the Churches such aid could only reinforce the advantage to the established Church. Their relative ineffectiveness in positive achievement in education, of which the handling of the situation in Lancashire is a prime example, condemned nonconformity to the infinitely less attractive and useful alternative of what could be construed as obstructive moral posturing. Nowhere was this more clearly seen than in their retreat into voluntaryism and their campaign against the 1902 Education Act as they attacked with words and by an appeal to principles a situation of which their own earlier inactivity was in large part the cause. As Professor Best has observed in this regard, the consideration of religious conflict in English education in the early part of the nineteenth century 'suggests that the religious education of the nation cannot be ensured without the supremacy of one Church and the State's strict regard for its doctrines ' [122]. The roots of that supremacy lay in the hard practicalities of organizational and financial strength at the local level. These rather than any prescriptive right gave the Establishment its hard won victory over nonconformity from which, up to 1914, so much recrimination and suspicion was the outcome.

Notes

I am grateful to Canon G.D. Leonard and Canon R.T. Holtby of the National Society and to Mr K.E. Priestley, the Principal of the Borough Road College, Isleworth for permission to use and quote from the private papers of the National and British Societies referred to here and for their allowing the various illustrative items presented here to be photographed and published.

1 Lawrence Stone, 'Literacy and Education in England 1640-1900', *Past and Present* (February 1969). Michael Sanderson, 'Literacy and Social Mobility in the Industrial Revolution'. *Past and Present* (August 1972).
2 National Society Letter Files (henceforth N.S.L.F.), Bottom Gate, Letter J.W. Whittaker to National Society (henceforth N.S.),6 April 1824.
3 N.S.L.F. Great Marsden. Letter J. Rushton to N.S., 16 May 1839.
4 Rev. F. Bennett, The Advantage of Sunday Schools (Manchester, 1785), p.4.

32 LOCAL STUDIES AND THE HISTORY OF EDUCATION

5 Rev. O. Sargent, *An Address* (Manchester, 1830), p.11.
6 C.J. Blomfield, *A Sermon at the Yearly Meeting of the Children of the Charity Schools* (London, 1827?), pp.7, 14. See also his *Remonstrance addressed to H. Brougham Esq., M.P.* (London, 1823). Hon. and Rev. Horace Powys, *Secular and Religious Education* (Warrington, 1839), p.10.
7 Rev. Samuel Waddy, *The Importance and Obligation of Early Religious Education* (Manchester, 1838).
8 *Annual Account of the S.P.C.K.* 1750. (S.P.C.K. Archives.)
9 W.E.Tate, 'The S.P.C.K. Archives', *Archives III* (Michaelmas 1957), Appendix II.
10 Cheshire County Record Office. Call and Exhibition Books, Manchester, Warrington, Blackburn and Leyland deaneries, 1783 and 1804. See also W.E.Tate, 'The Episcopal Licensing of Schoolmasters in England', *Church Quarterly Review* (Oct.-Dec. 1956), pp. 426 ff.
11 Owen Chadwick, *The Victorian Church* (London, 1970), Pt I, pp. 168, 158. Olive Brose, *Church and Parliament 1828-60* (Stanford, 1959), Chapter IX.
12 N.S.L.F. Flaxmoss. Letter W. Gray to N.S., 24 February 1838. See also files for Grane, Heywood, Lower Darwen, Clifton, Preston St Mary for similar motives and fears.
13 N.S.L.F. Rawtenstall. Letter J. Rushton to N.S., 10 April 1838.
14 National Society General Committee MS Minutes, 16 Oct. 1811. See also H.J.Burgess, *Enterprise in Education* (London: S.P.C.K., 1958). C.F.K.Brown, *The Church's Part in Education* (London: S.P.C.K., 1942). W.O.B.Allen and Edmund McClure, *Two Hundred Years, the History of the Society for Promoting Christian Knowledge 1698-1898* (London: S.P.C.K., 1898).
15 National Society General Minute, 8 April 1812.
16 *First Report of the National Society*, p.30.
17 *Second Report of the National Society*, p.98.
18 *Fourth Report of the National Society*, pp. 59 ff. See also Lancashire County Record Office (L.C.R.O.), DDPr/138/22, *Report of the Committee for Establishing a School at Preston*, Preston, 30 Dec. 1814.
19 A fragment of this circular issued by Bishop Law in 1814 was discovered among some uncatalogued scraps in the Cheshire County Record Office. There was no trace of the full series of replies.
20 General Minutes, 13 January 1830.
21 *Twenty First Report*, p.99.
22 Broadsheet, 4 Dec. 1812, by Rev. J. Dogson; in Blackburn Public Library.
23 L.C.R.O. PR/1551, MS Minutes of the National and Sunday Schools in Blackburn 1829-43. See for example 9 Nov. 1830 and 13 Dec. 1831.
24 L.C.R.O. PR/1549/6, Coucher Book of Billinge Schools; PR/

1549/31, Couchei Book of Walton-le-Dale; PR/1549/6, Coucher Book of Witton. Whittaker kept all his trivial correspondence with these schools in his district.
25 PR/1549/18/1, Letter and Resolution, Bishop J.B.Sumner to Dr Whittaker.
26 PR/1549/18/2, Letter and Notice H.Powys to Dr Whittaker.
27 T.C.Foster, *A Verbatim Report of the Great Diocesan Meeting at Warrington* (Warrington, 1839). See also *Liverpool Mail*, 26 January 1839.
28 PR/1549/18/7, Meeting of the Amounderness Deanery, 21 February 1839.
29 *Wigan Gazette,* 12 April 1839, for example, for the St Helens meeting.
30 *Report of the Chester Diocesan Board of Education,* 1839.
31 David Salmon, *Joseph Lancaster* (London, 1904). H. Bryan Binns, *A Century of Education 1808-1908* (London, 1908). *An Account of the Progress of Joseph Lancaster's Plan for the Education of Poor Children. Report of J. Lancaster's Progress from the Year 1798 with the Report of the Finance Committee for the Year 1810.* British Museum Add. MS 27823. Place MSS 'Lancasterian Schools' for this early history.
32 James Murphy, 'The Rise of Public Elementary Education in Liverpool, Pt.I 1784 1818', *Transactions of the Historic Society of Lancashire and Cheshire,* Vol.116 (1964). Dr Murphy suggests that Lancaster visited the city in 1806 and 1809. However a set of handbills advertising Lancaster's meetings suggests that he was there in 1808 also. See Friends' House, London, where the handbills are in Pamphlets 073.7.
33 C.W.Ethelston, *Address . . . to a General Meeting* (Manchester, 1811), p.12.
34 *Memoir of Benjamin Braidley Esq.* (London, 1845), p.122.
35 Joseph Aston, *A Picture of Manchester* (Manchester, 1816), p.143.
36 British and Foreign Schools Society Miscellaneous MSS (at the Borough Road College). Letter 18 July 1809, William Wilberforce to a Lady in Lancaster (Mrs Ford?).
37 *An Historical and Descriptive Account of the Town of Lancaster* (Lancaster, 1807). MS marginal note p.51 in the copy in Dr. Shepherd's Library, Preston.
38 *Report from the Select Committee . . . Education for the Children of the Poorer Classes.* Evidence of Henry Dunn, Q.384 p.50; B.P.P. 1837-8 (589) vii.
39 *Blackburn Mail,* 6 March 1811.
40 N.S.L.F. for Milnrow, Harpurhey, Lathom, Bamber Bridge for examples of this.
41 J.B.Sumner's Primary and Triennial Visitation Charges were published in 1829, 1832, 1835, 1838.
42 S.E.Maltby, *Manchester and the Movement for National Elementary Education 1800-1870* (Manchester, 1918). J.Murphy, *The*

Religious Problem in English Education (Liverpool, 1959).
43 T.P.Bunting, *The Life of Jabez Bunting, D.D.* (London, 1859), 2 vols. W.Gordon Robinson, *William Roby 1766-1830* (London, 1954). T.Taylor, *A Memoir of Mr Joseph Harbottle* (1866).
44 The Subscription List to the Queen's Letter Fund is in the 1839 Report pp.lxxi-ii.
45 Calculated from the yearly lists of grants in the Annual Reports. The dates refer to the date of the report in which the grant is listed.
46 *Annual Report* for 1839, Appendix VIII, pp.90-1. The year-by-year totals in the preceding reports detailing receipt of Treasury grants are not wholly accurate.
47 *Reports of the Royal Lancasterian Free School Manchester,* 1815-19, 1823-7, 1838-9, 1839-40. MS Minute Book of the British School Rochdale (in Rochdale Public Library) and *Reports of the Rochdale Auxiliary British and Foreign School Society,* 1835, 1836, 1839.
48 *Blackburn Mail,* 1 August 1827.
49 Calculated from a collation of (a) *Report of the Royal Lancasterian School Manchester,* 1827 (b) *Report of the Manchester and Salford Co-operating Society . . . Education of the Poor,* 1830 (c) *Pigot's Directory,* 1830.
50 Sponsors of the British School Bolton – 6 spinners, 2 muslin manufacturers, 1 linen draper, 1 wine merchant, 1 bleacher, 2 tea dealers, 1 tobacco manufacturer, 1 corn dealer, 2 gentlemen, 1 railway company treasurer, 1 tanner, 1 bootmaker, 1 gun maker, 1 brass founder, 4 unknown. Calculated from MS Letter Memorial, 28 March 1835, Ministry of Education Treasury Files, Vol. Ty. 1 Box 135, Folio 593.
51 *Report of the Chester Diocesan Board of Education,* 1839.
52 National Society General Committee Minutes, 15 January 1812.
53 Calculated from National Society, MS School Minutes, 7 vols, 1812-39.
54 N.S.L.F. Chester Diocesan. Letter T.Armistead to N.S., 26 March 1812.
55 *Report of the State of the Diocesan School in Chester,* 1812-17.
56 *Report of the State of the Diocesan School in Chester,* 1817-18.
57 Lancaster National School, MS Minutes, Vol.2, 10 July 1821.
58 National Society Annual Reports, List of Schools 1815, pp.108, 110, and 1818, p. 138; also 1830, p. 90.
59 The modern training college was the product of the later movement of 1839, and no trace of the earlier attempt is retained there. I am grateful to the former Principal for correspondence on this point.
60 *Reports of the Society for Bettering the Conditions and Increasing the Comforts of the Poor,* Vol.6, 1814. Article on the Barrington School.
61 Accrington National School, MS Minutes, 27 January 1818. (By courtesy of Rev. A.C. Wood.)

62 Lancaster National School, MS Minutes, 6 February 1824.
    (Lancaster Library).
63 Ibid. 28 October 1815.
64 Ibid. 13 December 1827.
65 Lancaster National School Annual Report, 1834.
66 Gregson MSS, Liverpool Record Office, Letter Books, Vol.2,
    items 21 and 36, Letters T.C.Dod to Matthew Gregson, 18
    November 1816 and 1 December 1816.
67 C.C.Southey, *The Life of the Rev. Andrew Bell* (London, 1844),
    Vol.3, p.447. Letter Mr Forster to Bell, 2 September 1831.
68 N.S.L.F. Liverpool. Letter Rev. A. Campbell to N.S., 29 June
    1839.
69 Lancaster National School. Minute, 9 December 1819.
70 Ibid. Minute, 2 November 1827.
71 N.S.L.F. Warrington. Letter, Horace Powys to N.S., 23 January
    1834.
72 *National Society Annual Report*, 1830. List of Schools, p.62.
    Manchester is in capitals as a central school.
73 National Society School Committee Minutes, 21 September 1837.
74 N.S.L.F. Warrington. Horace Powys to N.S., 12 December 1838.
75 MS Register of Masters 1804-21 (at the Borough Road College).
76 MS Register of Schoolmistresses, 1806-27.
77 Andrew Bell, *The Elements of Tuition* (London, 1813), espec-
    ially Pt.I, pp.33-43; Pt.II, pp.212-71. Thomas Bernard, *The New
    School* (London, 1809).
78 Joseph Lancaster, *Improvements in Education* (London, 1803),
    especially pp.53 ff.
79 Joseph Fox, *A Comparative View of the Plans of Education as
    Detailed in the Publications of Dr Bell and Mr Lancaster* (London,
    1808). For an interesting discussion of method in relation to
    school architecture and fittings see Malcolm Seaborne, *The
    English School, its Architecture and Organization 1370-1870*
    (London, 1971), Chapter VIII.
80 Report of the Warrington National and Sunday Schools, 1838, p.5.
81 Sibson Papers, Warrington Library, MS/739, Specimen Monitors'
    Exercises.
82 *Twenty Fourth Annual Report of the National Society, 1835.*
    Report from Wigan, p.61.
83 Job Pippins, *A Discursive View . . . of a Sermon on the Nature
    and Object of National Education* (Warrington, 1836).
84 *British and Foreign School Society Report*, 1818, p.15.
85 Broadsheet 'To the Public . . . a Sufferer' (Liverpool, 1814) and
    *Fifteenth Annual Report of the Day and Sunday Schools in
    Circus Street, Liverpool*, 1817-18.
86 *British and Foreign School Society Report*, 1839. Report from
    Bolton, p.53.
87 Ibid. 1818. Report from Lancaster, p.106.
88 Ibid. 1815. Report from Manchester, p.77.

89 *Report of the Warrington National and Sunday Schools*
    (Warrington, 1838), p.5.
90 National Society, MS General Minutes, 16 June 1813.
91 National Society, MS School Committee Minutes, 30 July 1813.
92 N.S.L.F. Bury. Letter H. Unsworth to N.S., 29 April 1814.
93 School Committee Minutes, 7 April 1815.
94 Ibid. 2 September 1814.
95 Ibid. 1 December 1815.
96 Ibid. 29 March 1816.
97 Southey, op. cit. Vol. II, p.418. Bell to Rev. William Johnson,
    2 August 1812.
98 Ibid. p.415. Bell to Johnson, July 1812.
99 Ibid. pp.418-19. Bell to Kenyon, 1812.
100 Ibid. p.673. Bell to Kenyon, 2 August 1813.
101 Ibid. p.492. Bell to Kenyon, 1814.
102 Ibid. p.678 (misprinted as 687). Bell to Kenyon, 26 Jan. 1814.
103 Southey, op.cit. Vol.III, pp.1-2. Bell to Kenyon.
104 N.S.L.F. Everton St Augustin. Letter J. Banks to N.S., 25 October
    1814.
105 Southey, op.cit. Vol III, p.33.
106 Ibid. pp.65-7.
107 Ibid. Dr Briggs to Bell.
108 Ibid. p.287.
109 Ibid. p.294.
110 Ibid. p.335.
111 Ibid. p.494.
112 N.S.L.F. Downham. Letter T.Abbott to N.S., 27 November 1839.
113 N.S.L.F. Rough Lee. Letter J.Rushton to N.S., 29 December 1838.
114 *British and Foreign School Society Report*, 1817, p.41.
115 William Allen, *The Life of William Allen with Selections from
    His Correspondence*, 3 vols (London, 1846). The exception is in
    Vol.II, p.235.
116 *Rochdale Recorder*, 3 February 1827.
117 *Report*, 1831, p.34.
118 *Report*, 1838, p.75 refers to this 1835 activity.
119 *Manchester Athenaeum List of Lectures 1835-1886* (Manchester,
    1888), p.212.
120 Henry Ashworth, *Recollections of Richard Cobden M.P.* (London,
    1876), p.16.
121 Gillian Sutherland, *Elementary Education in the Nineteenth
    Century,* Historical Association Pamphlet (London, 1971), p.16.
122 G.F.A.Best, 'The Religious Difficulties of National Education in
    England 1800-70', *Cambridge Historical Journal,* Vol.XII, No.2
    (1956).

ALAN EVERITT

Nonconformity in
the Victorian countryside

At the height of their power, in the middle of the nineteenth century, dissenters probably comprised nearly half the churchgoing population of England [1]. In the north-eastern counties, Cornwall, Wales and parts of the Midlands they actually numbered more than half [2]. It has long seemed to me, as a student of local society in England, that it is impossible to make any valid assessment of provincial life during the last three centuries without taking some account of nonconformist development. In the company of educational historians I do not need to labour this point. Yet till relatively recent years little detailed attention has been paid by academic scholars to the subject, apart from vague allusions to 'the nonconformist conscience' and 'radical nonconformity' [3].

The importance of dissent in provincial life has, however, long been recognized outside academic circles and has, indeed, given rise to a very considerable literature of a kind. It must be confessed, however, that, faced with the older chapel histories and dissenting hagiographies, even the most intrepid historian with no *a priori* interest in the subject is apt to wilt. This paper will make no attempt to synthesize this work or to explore the deeper spiritual problems of dissenting history. It sets out with the more limited aim of answering a single elementary question: in what types of rural community did dissent tend to find a foothold and flourish? Was there any relationship between the differing species of local society and the proliferation of dissent in certain well-defined areas, or its relative absence in others [4]? The further question of whether there was any relationship between these various kinds of dissenting settlement and differences in rural education is one that I must leave to historians of education to tackle. It is a question that might well be worth exploring in some detail in different parts of the country.

37

I

In a recent paper I tried to relate the distribution of dissent in its earlier phases, before the Evangelical Revival, to these varying forms of local society [5]. I now want to trace a similar relationship at a later date, namely in the mid-nineteenth century, after the impact of Evangelicalism had revolutionized the place of nonconformity in English life. The most obvious fact about nonconformity in the nineteenth century is that it was altogether different in scale from nonconformity in the seventeenth. At the time of the Compton Census in 1676, dissenters seem to have numbered no more than six or seven per cent of the population. True, the 1670s were a period of persecution, and the Compton Census has serious limitations as a historical source. Yet the general tenor of the evidence suggests that, with some notable exceptions, most nonconformist groups remained relatively small and sparse until at least the middle of the eighteenth century. They exerted an influence in English society out of all proportion to their modest numbers; yet the days of great 'revivals' and mass conversions still lay in the future [6].

By the 1850s dissenters were not only far more numerous in absolute numbers than before, but had come to form a far larger proportion of the population. This is clear from the census of 1851, which was the first and only one to record religious allegiance, and which forms the basic source for the present paper [7]. This census is a most interesting document, but it has several grave limitations as a statistical source. It does not tell us what we should most like to know, namely the actual number of members attached to each church and chapel in 1851. What it does tell us is:

(a)   the number of churches and chapels in each parish;
(b)   the number of 'sittings' in each church and chapel;
(c)   the number of people who attended each service on Census Sunday.

At first sight the last figure, that of attendants, may seem the most useful; but for various reasons it is in fact an unreliable and difficult one to interpret. Although the other figures, for churches, chapels and 'sittings', are also subject to obvious limitations, I have felt it safer to base my paper chiefly upon these [8]. In the four counties principally studied for this paper (Leicestershire, Lincolnshire, Northamptonshire and Kent) they do not seem likely to be seriously misleading. When the census tells us that there were 221 Primitive Methodist chapels in Lincolnshire with 25,164 sittings, but only 16 in Northamptonshire with 1,759 sittings, we need not assume that these figures exactly represent the local strength of Primitive Methodism; but they do furnish a rough guide to its comparative predominance and point up important differences between the two counties.

Throughout the following study Roman Catholics and Jews have been excluded. Both groups are special cases and as a rule they formed at this date a very small minority of the population. Their inclusion would not, in fact, have materially affected the statistics. The 'sittings' for the two bodies respectively in the four counties were: Kent 3,337 Roman Catholics (13 places of worship) and 315 Jews (5 places of worship); Leicestershire 2,537 (12) and nil; Lincolnshire 2,019 (13) and nil; Northamptonshire 705 (6) and nil. Roman Catholics thus formed 1 per cent of the churchgoing population in Kent (judged by number of 'sittings'), 1.6 per cent in Leicestershire, 0·7 per cent in Lincolnshire, and 0.5 per cent in Northamptonshire. Traditionally Lancashire is always thought of as a 'Catholic' county, and it was certainly more so than any other. But in 1851 there were in fact only 55,610 Roman Catholic 'sittings' in the county, compared with 324,751 nonconformists and 383,466 Anglicans. In this case, it is true, the figures may well be a somewhat misleading guide to the strength of Catholicism; yet it is difficult to deny that even in Lancashire Catholics must have been outnumbered by both Congregationalists (80,072 sittings) and Wesleyan Methodists (107,983 sittings).

With the limitations of the census in mind, what do the 1851 figures tell us? The first point is that, judged by the number of sittings, 44 per cent of the churchgoing population as a whole at this time were dissenters, and 56 per cent Anglicans (see Table 1). The census figures probably in some areas considerably exaggerated the strength of Anglicanism, particularly in the eastern counties where there were many large parish churches serving small or dwindling populations. In Norfolk and Suffolk particularly the numbers of 'sittings' probably overstress the strength of Anglicanism by a considerable margin. It is quite possible that dissenters may have formed half, or nearly half, the population in these two counties. But at any rate the outstanding fact to notice is the enormous growth of nonconformity since the late seventeenth century, when it comprised probably no more than 6 or 7 per cent of the population as a whole.

The second point about the census figures is the striking regional

Table 1   *General Religious Allegiance in 1851*

		Total Church and Chapel Sittings	Anglicans		Dissenters	
			Sittings	%	Sittings	%
1	Herefordshire	68,675	49,312	72	19,363	28	41
2	Rutland	17,299	12,131	70	5,168	30	40
3	Oxfordshire	109,301	74,369	68	34,932	32	39
4	Sussex	160,011	108,076	67	51,935	33	38
5	Surrey	219,094	143,783	66	75,311	34	37
6	Westmorland[1]	37,239	24,411	66	12,828	34	36
7	Dorset	120,082	77,886	65	42,196	35	35
8	Kent	299,296	194,443	65	104,853	35	34
9	Hampshire	212,161	135,720	64	76,441	36	33
10	Shropshire	143,663	92,435	64	51,228	36	32
11	Suffolk[2]	224,229	141,417	63	82,812	37	31
12	Middlesex	552,231	344,487	62	207,744	38	30
13	Berkshire	92,737	56,679	61	36,058	39	29
14	Essex	216,113	132,041	61	84,072	39	28
15	Somerset	287,353	174,723	61	112,630	39	27
16	Warwickshire	201,831	123,624	61	78,207	39	26
17	Worcestershire	138,668	85,155	61	53,513	39	25
18	Norfolk[2]	283,420	168,722	60	114,698	40	24
19	Hertfordshire	93,230	55,193	59	38,037	41	23
20	Devon	332,934	191,710	58	141,224	42	22
21	Staffordshire	279,516	161,217	58	118,299	42	21
22	Buckinghamshire	113,209	64,231	57	48,978	43	20
23	Cumberland	99,783	56,803	57	42,980	43	19
24	Gloucestershire	276,606	156,651	57	119,955	43	18
25	Northamptonshire	150,472	84,816	56	65,656	44	17
26	Wiltshire	158,694	87,843	55	70,851	45	16
27	Lancashire	708,217	383,466	54	324,751	46	15
28	Cheshire	229,711	121,882	53	107,829	47	14
29	Leicestershire	156,678	82,964	53	73,714	47	13
30	Huntingdonshire	45,014	23,568	52	21,446	48	12
31	Cambridgeshire	104,196	52,917	51	51,279	49	11
32	Lincolnshire	279,247	142,844	51	136,403	49	10
33	North Riding	161,062	79,740	50	81,322	50	9
34	Bedfordshire	87,814	42,557	48	45,257	52	8
35	Derbyshire	182,581	87,829	48	94,752	52	7
36	Nottinghamshire	150,024	70,928	47	79,096	53	6
37	East Riding	140,793	64,135	46	76,658	54	5
38	West Riding	665,428	276,910	42	388,518	58	4
39	Co. Durham	167,285	66,319	40	100,966	60	3
40	Northumberland	131,646	52,405	40	79,241	60	2
41	Cornwall	261,684	95,155	36	166,529	64	1
	TOTAL	8,359,227	4,641,497	56	3,717,730	44	

differences in the pattern of dissent that they indicate. These differences also need some care, however, in interpretation. At a first glance, the analysis of religious allegiance in Table 1 seems to suggest two principal and not unfamiliar tendencies in this pattern. In the first place nonconformity appears to have been more powerful in the north than in the south. In the whole of the north-east, from Derbyshire and Nottinghamshire up to the Scottish border, dissenters apparently comprised more than half the communicant population, and in Durham and Northumberland as much as 60 per cent of it [9]. In the counties south of the Thames, by contrast, nonconformists generally appear to have formed little more than one-third of the population. Secondly, dissenters often appear to have been more strongly represented in industrial than in agricultural counties. Nine of the ten counties with the highest percentage of Anglicans — about two-thirds of the churchgoing population — were predominantly agrarian, namely Herefordshire, Rutland, Oxfordshire, Shropshire, Westmorland, Dorset, Hampshire, Sussex and Kent. In counties with a good deal of industry, like Yorkshire, Derbyshire, Nottinghamshire and Durham, by contrast, they formed less than half the population.

These overall tendencies certainly cannot be ignored: there is undoubtedly some truth in them; but the more closely they are examined, the more unsatisfactory they appear as generalizations. To some extent the disparities between different counties were merely due to the fact that Anglican churches tended, for historical reasons, to be more numerous in the south than the far north. West of the Pennines, moreover, in contrast with the east, dissenters nowhere formed as much as half the population, and in Westmorland the proportion was exceptionally small (34 per cent). In Staffordshire and Lancashire, two of the most industrial counties in England, the nonconformist proportion, though high, was markedly lower (namely 42 per cent and 46 per cent) than in highly agrarian counties like Huntingdonshire, Cambridgeshire and Bedfordshire where it ranged from 48 to 52 per cent [10]. In the predominantly agricultural North and East Ridings the proportion of dissenters, though lower than in the West Riding, was still remarkably high by national standards, amounting

Notes to Table 1

1 The number of sittings in the four Baptist chapels in the county was not reported. These have been estimated at 1,000.

2 The figures for Anglican sittings in these counties are probably affected by the exceptional size and number of ancient parish churches.

to more than half the churchgoing population. Finally, we must not forget that absolute numbers may in some respects be as significant as percentages in assessing the strength of dissent. And these show that of the 13 counties with more than 100,000 chapel sittings in 1851, eight were in the south and only five in the north, whilst four were predominantly industrial and seven or eight at this date predominantly agrarian: Kent, Somerset, Norfolk, Devon, Gloucestershire, Lincolnshire, Cheshire and Cornwall. The fact is, I think, that it is first of all essential to examine *local* differences in the distribution of dissent — *differences between various types of parish* — before generalizing about large-scale *regional* differences between the counties. With some important exceptions, this has been unduly neglected in the study of nonconformity hitherto.

The third point to note about nonconformity in the mid-nineteenth century is its astonishing fissiparation into warring factions. True, the great majority of dissenters (in most counties more than 95 per cent) belonged to one or other of the more orthodox branches of the three principal denominations — Congregationalists, Baptists and Methodists. Yet at no previous period, not even during the Great Rebellion, had there been such an extraordinary plethora of sects as in the mid-Victorian era. At the end of 1866 there were no fewer than 98 religious denominations recorded in the register of marriages in England and Wales, and even this figure did not include all that were known to exist. The variety of these sects and their vivid nomenclature come as something of an eye-opener. What exactly, one wonders, can have been the distinguishing tenets of such bodies as the Hallelujah Band, the Christian Eliasites, the New Jerusalem Church, the Peculiar People, the Progressivists, the Recreative Religionists, the Wesleyan Reform Glory Band, and the Christians who Object to be Otherwise Designated? In a sceptical and self-conscious age, such oddities must provoke a certain amount of mirth. Yet it would be a mistake not to sense behind the absurdity something of significance. Such fissiparation, after all, underlines, at a certain social level, the restlessness of the Victorian conscience.

The fourth point to notice about mid-Victorian dissent was its strength in the country districts of England. I do not mean to say that it was not also strong in many of the great cities. Outside London it certainly was. But the common idea that Victorian nonconformity, like Tudor and Stuart Puritanism, was essentially an urban phenomenon is not borne out by the facts. True, it was more urbanized in some counties than in others: curiously enough it was exceptionally urban in the predominantly agricultural county of Kent. Yet nearly two-thirds of the 841 dissenting chapels in Northamptonshire and Lindsey at this time (to take two not untypical areas) were in country parishes, not in towns, and in Leicestershire the rural proportion was nearly 70 per cent. Most rural chapels, admittedly, were smaller than those in towns; yet the strength of dissent in the countryside over most of England in 1851 cannot seriously be questioned.

In order to elucidate further the factors in this strength of the rural element in Victorian nonconformity I have selected these four counties for more detailed study, that is to say Leicestershire, Northamptonshire, Lindsey and Kent. The strength of dissent varied considerably between them. In Lincolnshire, almost half the churchgoing population were then nonconformists. This was an exceptionally high proportion, exceeded only in Cornwall, Bedfordshire and the north-eastern counties, though it was nearly equalled in Leicestershire and a few other shires with a figure of 47 or 48 per cent. Despite the extraordinary number of medieval parishes in Lincolnshire - more than 600 - there were in fact many more dissenting chapels there in the mid-nineteenth century than Anglican churches, to be precise 831 to 657. In Victorian Kent, by contrast, nonconformists numbered little more than a third of the churchgoing population (35 per cent), whereas Anglicans comprised nearly two-thirds (see Table 1).

There were many other differences in the pattern of dissent between these four counties, such as (for example) the remarkable strength of the Old Dissent in Northamptonshire and its weakness in Lindsey. But I do not propose to discuss these differences in any detail. What I do want to concentrate on is the equally striking resemblances in the pattern of dissent as between the four shires. No English county, of course, is entirely homogeneous in its forms of parochial society. Each shire comprises a number of diverse sub-regions or rural economies within it, and a varied spectrum of parish-types. Now in each of the four counties under consideration there coexisted a somewhat similar spectrum of parish types and some at least of the same kinds of rural economy. And the significant fact is that in each of the four counties dissent tended to be associated chiefly with certain forms of local society, while it was largely absent from others.

What relation did the new pattern of dissent in these four counties in the 1850s bear to the original pattern of dissent in the seventeenth century? Very often it was associated with the same forms of rural economy as before. In Kent and Sussex, for instance, the Weald remained, as it had been in the seventeenth century, the classic area of local nonconformity. In fact forest societies like the Weald elsewhere also continued to encourage dissent. As early as 1661 it had been said that 'the Wild of Kent is a receptacle for distressed running parsons, who vent abundance of sedition' [11]; and in the nineteenth century dissent remained powerful in the old Wealden centres like Cranbrook, Staplehurst and Tenterden. By 1851, however, dissenters were also numerous in quite different types of local community from the woodland settlements. In Kent they were now also powerful in a number of downland parishes like Elham and Meopham. At the time of the Compton Census in 1676 there had been only one downland parish in the whole of Kent (Ripple, near Dover) with more than 20 nonconformists; by 1851 chapels had sprung up in many others, and in a few there were two or three. One of the interesting facts about many of these newly dissenting parishes in 1851 was that they were early centres of primary settlement and were two or three times as large in area as the normal dowland parish. This indicates important differences in their social structure and history which go far to explain their dissenting proclivities. In east Leicestershire, too, where dissent had hitherto been comparatively weak, Methodist chapels had been established by 1851 in many country parishes. Most striking of all was the difference in a county like Lincolnshire. This was an area with no considerable forest tracts, and, it seems, comparatively little dissent before the eighteenth century. Yet by 1851 dissenters had come close to outnumbering Anglicans. How can we explain this new layer in the palimpsest of nonconformity? In what types of rural parish and of rural economy had the New Dissent in fact taken root?

II

Glancing one day through the pages of the *Imperial Gazetteer,* published in 1870, I noticed almost by chance that dissenting chapels often seemed to be associated with parishes where the property was described as 'divided' or 'much subdivided', i.e. between numerous landowners [12]. The information about dissent in the *Gazetteer* was based upon the census of 1851, and that about property-holding upon the return of 1860. This chance observation led to a more thorough investigation of the relationship between patterns of landownership and the distribution of dissent in the four counties already mentioned.

The resemblances and contrasts between them prove to be quite remarkable.

Altogether there were 1,343 parishes in these four counties, but for 111 of them the information about landownership was inadequate, and these had to be omitted. The analysis of the remaining 1,232 parishes is summarized in Table 2. Broadly speaking, the property in each parish is described in the return as either 'in one hand', 'in a few hands', 'sub divided' or 'much subdivided'. For the sake of simplicity in the present argument the two former classes may be broadly grouped together under the name of 'estate parishes', since in these all the land appears to have been held by a single magnate or a few dominant landowners; whilst the two latter classes, where land was divided amongst many proprietors, may be grouped under the designation 'freeholders' parishes', since they evidently contained many small and independent owners [13]. This rough and ready division obviously glosses over with deceptive simplicity what was in fact a highly complex pattern of landownership. But for a generalized survey like the present a minute examination of the structure of landowning in more than 1,200 parishes would have been impracticable.

Within the economy of each of the four counties, the predominant influence of landownership upon the spread of nonconformity is very evident. Table 2 analyses the parishes in each shire by *type of property-holding*. The third division of the table, headed 'Total of I and II', represents all the 'estate parishes', where there was a single landlord or a few dominant squires. In Kent 86 per cent of these estate parishes had no dissenting chapel of any kind: in only 14 per cent was there any organized nonconformity. In Lindsey the position was similar to that in Kent, with chapels in only 18 per cent of the estate parishes. In Northamptonshire and Leicestershire the absence of dissent in this type of community was not quite so striking, yet there too there was no organized nonconformity in about three-quarters of these estate parishes. In all four counties, then, nonconformist chapels were very much the exception wherever land was concentrated in the hands of a few local magnates. In the case of parishes where all the land was controlled by a *single* magnate, dissent hardly ever established a foothold. In only three of the 119 parishes in this category was there any form of organized nonconformity.

Further down the table the section headed 'Total of III and IV' comprises all the 'freeholders' parishes', that is where land was 'sub-divided' or 'much subdivided' amongst many small, independent

Table 2   *Landholding and rural dissent in four counties, c.1860.*
(Figures in percentages)

Type of Parish	(a) No Chapel	(b) One Chapel	(c) Two Chapels	(d) Three or more Chapels	Total of (b),(c) and (d)
I Property in one hand					
Kent	-	-	-	-	-
Lindsey	97	1.5	-	1.5	3
Leicestershire	100	3	-	-	-
Northamptonshire	97	3	-	-	3
II Property in a few hands					
Kent	86	10	3	1	14
Lindsey	74	16	8	2	26
Leicestershire	68	25	6	1	32
Northamptonshire	71	21	7	1	29
Total of I and II					
Kent	86	10	3	1	14
Lindsey	82	11	5	2	18
Leicestershire	73	21	5	1	27
Northamptonshire	75	18	6	1	25
III Property subdivided					
Kent	52	46	2	-	48
Lindsey	12	35	41	12	88
Leicestershire	18	50	20	12	82
Northamptonshire	22	40	31	7	78
IV Property much subdivided					
Kent	17	56	19	8	83
Lindsey	15	19	36	30	85
Leicestershire	15	28	16	41	85
Northamptonshire	24	29	31	16	76
Total of III and IV					
Kent	30	53	12	5	70
Lindsey	14	25	38	23	86
Leicestershire	17	39	18	26	83
Northamptonshire	23	35	31	11	77
All types of parish					
Kent	61	29	7	3	39
Lindsey	53	17	19	11	47
Leicestershire	45	30	12	13	55
Northamptonshire	58	24	14	4	42

1   In the case of Lindsey and Leicestershire the percentages include 'probable' as well as 'certain' parishes. The former comprise 37 per cent of the total of 374 in Lindsey and 26 per cent of the total of 250 in Leicestershire. In Kent and Northamptonshire the 'probable' percentage is negligible (out of 340 and 282 parishes respectively). For 30 parishes in Kent, 33 in Lindsey, 20 in Leicestershire and 28 in Northamptonshire, information is inadequate, and these have been excluded from the table.

proprietors. The contrast here is remarkable. In Kent there was at least one dissenting chapel in 70 per cent of these freeholders' parishes, and in 17 per cent of them there was more than one. In the more strongly nonconformist Midland counties the proportions were a good deal higher. In Northamptonshire chapels were to be found in 77 per cent of these freeholders' parishes, in Leicestershire in 83 per cent and in Lindsey in 86 per cent. As the table shows there were also many freeholders' parishes in these three counties with two or three chapels, and some with four or five. The most extreme example of this proliferation of dissent in a freeholders' parish was Haxey, in Lindsey, where in 1851 there were no fewer than twelve different Methodist chapels. Even by Lincolnshire standards this was extraordinary; but there were nearly forty other rural parishes in Lindsey with three or more nonconformist churches, and 33 in Leicestershire.

III

Though freeholders' parishes form perhaps the most obvious and numerous kind of rural society encouraging dissent, they cannot always be invoked to explain its spread. Another form of society in which it tended to flourish was the boundary settlement, situated on the frontier between two parishes. Places of this kind tended to be particularly frequent in old forest districts, where wasteland was more abundant; but they were not confined to woodlands. In Kent, where they were exceptionally numerous, they were to be found here and there in most parts of the county. In Elham, for instance, a large downland parish of East Kent, the boundary bisects no fewer than 13 subsidiary communities. Dissent was not found in more than a few boundary settlements of this kind, of course. Most of them have remained solitary farmsteads ever since their foundation. A number, however, at some period of their history gradually developed into populous rural communities in their own right. Many were situated on what was once common land, shared between two or three parishes, where jurisdictions were difficult to define and tended to come into dispute. Such conditions often fostered independent or (according to one's viewpoint) lawless behaviour; for in such a community it was always easy, on the approach of the parish constable, to claim that the inhabitants in question were not under *his* jurisdiction but that of the next parish.

Closely similar in character to these boundary settlements were those which sprang up on extra-parochial tracts and wastes, usually at a comparatively late date, often during the last two or three centuries. Typical of these were places like Lye Waste in Worcestershire. Lye Waste is a relatively modern settlement. It originated after parliamentary enclosure on the uncultivated waste of Lye village, and is said to have been 'settled by a numerous body of men, who acquired a right of separate freehold on the passing of an enclosure act . . .' It consisted chiefly of nail-makers and of cottagers employed in the local iron works and coal mines. By 1870 there were four dissenting chapels on Lye Waste [14]. This kind of association between an outlying settlement, independent cottagers, rural industry and nonconformist propensities is characteristic of many Midland villages like this in the early days of industrialization.

IV

Yet another form of local community which was particularly prone to dissent was the decayed market town. Such places were not absolutely distinct from the 'freeholders' parishes' or indeed from boundary settlements; for in most former markets landownership tended to be subdivided, and a number of towns had been founded on parish boundaries. Nevertheless, the spread of dissent in these decayed markets is sufficiently striking to deserve separate comment.

The decline of the smaller markets of England has been a persistent theme of provincial life since the later Middle Ages. By the early fourteenth century market rights of some sort had been granted to many hundreds of English places, probably to at least 1,500. By the early sixteenth century, however, fewer than half the medieval markets of England had managed to survive as trading centres, and in the 1670s there were no more than about 800 market towns and villages in the whole of England and Wales. In most counties numbers dropped once again during the eighteenth century and much of the nineteenth, and by the end of Queen Victoria's reign there were only about half as many active markets as in the seventeenth century. In Leicestershire, for example, the number had fallen from more than 30 in 1340 to no more than 13 in the 1670s and a mere seven in the 1880s.

Now although so many places declined as markets they did not, as a rule, die out completely as human communities. Most of the old market centres of England remained considerable villages even after their trading functions died out. They tended to remain populous rural settlements, usually with no local squire but a large number of indepen dent freeholders and an agrarian economy diversified by various local crafts and small industries. This kind of local society was in fact very characteristic of pre-industrial England, far more so than it is today and more so than is generally recognized.

In Leicestershire many of the larger villages of the county – Kibworth, Arnesby, Kegworth, Hallaton, Belton, Billesdon, Shepshed and Great Glen, for example – had once been small market towns. When they lost their trading functions, often in the late Middle Ages but sometimes not till the eighteenth century, they remained sizeable rural communities, and it was probably often because of over-population that they were driven to develop local industries, such as framework-knitting, during the eighteenth and nineteenth centuries. In Northamptonshire the same features are apparent, and many of the lacemaking and shoe-manufacturing villages of the county, like Brixworth and Finedon, probably owed their populousness in the eighteenth and nineteenth centuries to their original status as markets. In Kent nearly all the so-called 'villages' of the county are strictly speaking decayed market towns rather than true agricultural villages: Ightham, Wrotham, Charing, Elham, Yalding, Smarden, Wye and many others: all come within this category. There had been nearly 100 medieval market centres in Kent, but by Queen Victoria's reign more than 70 of these had relapsed into village status.

In the nineteenth century parishes of this kind were almost invariably amongst the chief strongholds of rural dissent. Virtually all had nonconformist chapels of some kind, most had more than one, and many had three or four. In Kent, for instance, there were 33 rural communities with two or more nonconformist chapels in 1851, and of these nine or ten had once been markets, and five others, such as Cranbrook, still existed as small country towns. In Northamptonshire and Leicestershire much the same situation obtained as in Kent. In the former county, where there were 51 rural communities with more than one chapel, four still existed as small towns, 11 were certainly decayed markets, and possibly six others came within the same category. In Leicestershire, where 62 rural parishes had two chapels or more in 1851, five were still small towns, 12 had certainly once been markets, and perhaps four others. Between 46 and 57 of the 146 rural parishes where dissent was strongest in these three counties, therefore, had once been market towns.

Quite why places of this kind encouraged nonconformity to such an extent is a question which only intensive examination of the history and social composition of each community and its chapels would answer. Certain general features may, however, be distinguished. The original grant of market status, and often of burgage rights, had attracted outsiders to these communities, increased their population and conferred a measure of freedom upon their inhabitants. When the burghal functions died out, the tenurial structure tended to survive; independent freeholders were still numerous, the communities remained populous, and no doubt a certain tradition of independence continued to shape their history. When they reverted to village status, therefore, they remained villages with a difference. Most of them retained their annual fairs till the nineteenth century. From the later seventeenth century onwards most of them, particularly in Leicestershire and Northamptonshire, developed crafts or industries of some kind, such as framework-knitting, lacemaking, cloth-weaving, and shoe-manufacturing, no doubt in order to employ an increasing surplus of population. For these and other reasons the inhabitants of decayed markets were better able than most countryfolk to preserve a certain independence of the squirearchy, and to please themselves, to some extent, in matters of religious opinion.

V

Another and better-known form of rural community where dissent flourished in Victorian times was the industrial village. Such places cannot be rigidly distinguished from the types of local society hitherto discussed. Still, industrial villages are a sufficiently distinct species to be discussed on their own. In the two Midland counties under review, they were particularly numerous in the nineteenth century. There were many places in Leicestershire and Northamptonshire with an industrial character at that time which now appear wholly rural.

In Leicestershire I have examined 61 rural parishes where industries provided one of the chief sources of livelihood, and in Northamptonshire 42. This is not a complete list; but these examples are enough to demonstrate the propensity of this type of community to dissent [15]. In these 103 parishes there were nearly 200 non-conformist chapels of various denominations (see Table 3). In Leicestershire there were, on the average, at least two chapels in every industrial village. In only 7 of the 61 was there no organized dissent; in 18 parishes there were three or four chapels and in one (Shepshed)

Table 3 *Industrial villages in Leicestershire and Northamptonshire: Number of Chapels (L = Leicestershire; N = Northamptonshire; T = Total)*

	Villages			Total Chapels		
	L	N	T	L	N	T
No chapel	7	7	14	0	0	0
One chapel	19	16	35	19	16	35
Two chapels	16	12	28	32	24	56
Three chapels	10	4	14	30	12	42
Four chapels	8	3	11	32	12	44
Five chapels	1	0	1	5	0	5
Total	61*	42†	103	118	64	182

* At least eleven of these had formerly been market centres, and probably six others.

† At least fourteen of these had formerly been market centres, and probably four others.

there were five. In Northamptonshire the tendency was less striking, but there also it was quite evident. All but seven of the 42 industrial parishes had dissenting chapels of some kind; 19 had at least two, and seven had three or four.

VI

Somewhat similar in character to these industrial villages were the new railhead and canal settlements of the nineteenth century. In these, too, dissent usually established a firm footing. Sometimes, as at Barnton on the Trent and Mersey Canal in Cheshire, virtually the whole community became dissenters, in this, as in many cases, Methodists [16].

In Kent there were several railhead settlements with a somewhat similar history. One was Paddock Wood in the Weald, an entirely new village which sprang up after the building of the first railway in the county, from Redhill to Dover, at its junction with the branch line to Maidstone. Paddocks or Parrocks was an old manorial estate which had passed through the hands of a succession of landed families in Kent, but there had apparently never been a village or hamlet on the site. The new railhead was astutely placed, however, and it rapidly developed into a sizeable community with the expansion of orchards and hop-gardens in the area. By 1860, with a population of nearly 900, the village was large enough to be formed into a separate chapelry, and there seem to have been at least two dissenting groups established within it [17].

The growth of places like Paddock Wood was conditioned not only by the railway but by the local development of intensive farming, principally in fruit and hops, which demanded a large labour force. Though in Kent, as elsewhere, most rural parishes remained static in population or declined during the latter half of the nineteenth century, there were a number of agricultural settlements in the county, like Paddock Wood, where population continued to expand because of this need for a large labour force, especially in orchards and hop-gardens. In a sense these agricultural labourers' settlements were the Kentish equivalent of the 'industrial' villages of Leicestershire and Northamptonshire: much of the local surplus of population did not need to migrate to the towns, but was able to find employment in the surrounding countryside, though in this case not in the workshops but on farms. Intensive farming communities of this kind seem to have encouraged dissent in much the same way as the industrial villages of the East Midlands. At East Peckham, for instance, a populous parish in the heart of the Wealden fruit and hop area, whose inhabitants increased by more than 1,000 between 1801 (1,327) and 1861 (2,341), there were at least two dissenting chapels by the latter date.

At Newington, situated amongst orchards and hopgrounds near Sittingbourne, and at Ash-by-Wingham, a few miles inland from Sandwich, very similar conditions obtained. In each parish the land was intensively farmed, a large labour force was employed, the population rose gradually throughout the nineteenth century, and Methodism or Congregationalism flourished [18].

VII

In the Midlands there were a number of dissenting parishes where none of the conditions hitherto described accounts for the presence of nonconformity. The significant feature about many of these remaining parishes in the Midlands is that they did not conform to the normal Midland type of nucleated settlement, but were abnormally large parishes consisting of a number of dispersed hamlets or subsidiary townships [19]. Nonconformity was often able to develop in these outlying hamlets precisely because they were remote from the parish church.

In Lincolnshire, for example, the parish of Bottesford, where there were two nonconformist groups, covered more than 5,000 acres and comprised five distinct townships. Corringham, where there were also two chapels, covered more than 6,000 acres and comprised four subsidiary hamlets. Broughton, with two chapels, extended to nearly 7,000 acres and included the subsidiary township of Castlethorpe as well as the hamlets of Manby and Gokewell. There were a number of other parishes of this kind in Lindsey whose history would repay further exploration. Several of those mentioned, such as Corringham and Broughton, appear to have been places of very early primary settlement, like the larger downland parishes of Kent referred to on an earlier page, and this may have partly accounted for their peculiarities.

In Leicestershire the parish of Nailstone covered nearly 4,000 acres and comprised the subsidiary settlements of Normanton-le-Heath and Barton-in-the-Beans, in each of which there was a nonconformist meeting-place. Church Langton, with at least one dissenting group, consisted of four distinct townships and covered more than 4,000 acres. Prestwold, where there were two chapels, comprised three hamlets and covered nearly 5,000 acres. Rothley, with three chapels, covered 5,500 acres and included five separate townships within its borders. Tilton and Breedon, with two chapels each, were smaller parishes — each a little over 3,000 acres — but these also comprised several distinct townships. Once again a number of the Leicestershire instances, for example Breedon and Tilton, were places of early primary settlement.

A somewhat similar pattern was repeated in Northamptonshire. In Potterspury parish, there was an Independent chapel at Yardley Gobion. an outlying village which had no church of its own till 1864. In Weedon Lois the Baptist chapel was at Weston, and in Blakesley at Woodend, both of which were subsidiary hamlets with no Anglican church. The parish of Pattishall comprised as many as six outlying hamlets — Astcote, Dalscote, Eastcote, Foster's Booth, Foxley and Catchem's End — and contained two nonconformist meeting-places, for Baptists and Primitive Methodists. These Northamptonshire parishes and others like them were in the wooded part of the county towards the Buckinghamshire and Oxfordshire borders. Their settlement pattern was a mixture of nucleated Midland villages and scattered forest hamlets not unlike those of the Weald of Kent.

VIII

In all three Midland counties there were a number of parishes where neither local industries nor scattered forms of settlement nor any of the other factors hitherto adduced seem to explain the presence of dissent. These remaining places were definitely estate parishes, but their distinguishing feature was that the landlord concerned did not live in the parish itself but was either an absentee or else resident in some other parish on his estate [20]. As a consequence, despite the concentration of land in a few hands, there was a certain degree of freedom for the local village folk from the immediate eye of their landlord. There were a number of dissenting chapels in east Leicestershire, for example, in the estate parishes of the Duke of Rutland and the Earl of Dysart: at Saltby, Sproxton, Plungar and Redmile, to mention a few by name. The significance of these places is that they were well away from the seats of the two landed families concerned, which were at Belvoir and Buckminster.

In the estate parishes of the squirearchy, as distinct from those of titled magnates of this calibre, it is worth noting, dissenting chapels seem to have been noticeably rarer. Sometimes, it is clear, manorial control was more vigilant on the smaller landed estates, covering perhaps one or two parishes, than on the far-flung domains of a peer like the Duke of Rutland. This tendency must not be overstressed, but it seems to have obtained in a number of counties. There can be little doubt that it was one reason for the weakness of rural nonconformity in parts of Kent, which in 1851 was still, as it had always been, a classic land of relatively small, indigenous squires. At this period the characteristic landed estate in Kent covered no more than 3,000-5,000 acres, and many were much smaller. The largest property in the county was that of Viscount Holmesdale, covering about 16,000 acres around Linton Place. This is a figure that may be compared with the 70,000-acre estates of the Duke of Rutland in the Midlands, of which more than 30,000 acres were in Leicestershire alone, and the 57,000-acre estate of the Earl of Yarborough in Lincolnshire [21].

IX

It is clear, then, that rural nonconformity in the mid-nineteenth century was associated with a wide spectrum of settlement types. What were the common elements, if any, between these varied forms of dissenting community? At the risk of considerable over-simplification they may be said to have been threefold. In the first place they were almost all marked by an unusual degree of freedom: freedom either in the sense of comprising many small freeholders, self-employed craftsmen and tradesmen, or some similarly independent group of inhabitants; or else freedom in the sense of being situated well away from the nearest parish church and in many cases far from any manor-house. Amongst the former places, that is those containing many small, relatively independent men, were the freeholders' parishes, the decayed markets, the industrial villages, and many villages with a large labour-force in areas of intensive farming. Amongst those places that were free in the sense of being remote from a parish church were the subsidiary or outlying hamlets of earlier centres of settlement, the boundary communities and places that sprang up on extra-parochial tracts like Lye Waste, and many squatters' communities or entirely new settlements connected with canals or railways, such as Barnton in Cheshire and Paddock Wood in Kent. In so far as dissent was associated with these subsidiary settlements and outlying hamlets, it follows that it was especially prolific, generally speaking, in areas of essentially scattered settlement like the Weald, Cornwall, Wales and much of the Pennines. Still, by 1851 it was by no means confined to areas where settlement was dispersed, for it was at least equally powerful in nucleated villages and decayed markets wherever these contained a sizeable number of independent freeholders, craftsmen or tradesmen.

The second characteristic common to many dissenting communities is more elusive and at first sight more surprising. This was the tendency for nonconformity to develop principally either in communities of *very early* Anglo-Saxon origin or in areas of *very late* post-Conquest settlement. This tendency is not universally apparent, but it was often a striking feature in the pattern of rural dissent. On the one hand many of the woodland areas where nonconformity flourished, such as the Weald, were regions of large parishes, predominantly late, post-Conquest colonization, and comparative freedom from manorial control. Still later were the squatters' communities of the sixteenth and seventeenth centuries with which dissent was associated, and the new industrial villages of the eighteenth and nineteenth centuries. On the other hand many of the decayed markets and 'open villages' where dissent proliferated seem to have originated as communal settlements of 'the folk' during the earliest phases of the Anglo-Saxon invasions. Certainly many strongly nonconformist settlements in Northamptonshire and

Kent, such as Oundle and Wye, were places that had originated at a very early period, sometimes as centres of an Anglo-Saxon 'tribe' or *regio*.

There is nothing really mysterious in the association of dissent with very early and very late settlements, or its relative absence from those of intermediate date. The social and economic structure of the very early Anglo-Saxon places was often inherently favourable to nonconformity. Certainly in Kent and probably in Leicestershire, Northamptonshire and Lindsey many of these early places had originated as *communal* settlements and throughout their history they have often remained large and populous parishes comprising a numerous body of independent freeholders. In some sense many of them have always remained local meeting-places, and for this reason too they tended to become the focal points of religious life. First, perhaps (as at Wye), they had originated as centres for the worship of a heathen deity; then they became (in many cases) minster churches of the Anglo-Saxon kingdoms; and finally (at a much later date) they developed as centres of Protestant nonconformity, partly because they were convenient meeting-places and partly because they contained many small freeholders. The settlements of intermediate date, by contrast, in Kent at least, tended to be small manorial parishes, usually originating in the later Anglo-Saxon era or occasionally not until the Conquest period, and founded by a single individual or family. In Kent they were not normally communal settlements as the earlier Anglo-Saxon centres had been. Their churches were in origin often manorial chapels established by the local lord, intimately associated with his hall and dependent upon his patronage. And throughout their history, speaking generally, the manorial parishes have tended to remain the preserve of an exclusive squirearchy and to have resisted the incursions of nonconformity.

A third general characteristic of rural dissent, at first sight a slightly odd one, may be more tentatively advanced. In three at least of the four counties under review there was a marked tendency for the Old Dissent of the Baptist and Congregationalist communions to prevail in forest and wood-pasture areas, with their large parishes and scattered forms of settlement, whilst the New Dissent of Methodism tended to predominate, sometimes to a remarkable extent, in the generally smaller and more arable parishes of the limestone and lias belts. This contrast was especially evident in Leicestershire and Kent. Before the rise of the New Dissent, rural nonconformity in Kent was largely confined to the Weald and adjacent chartlands, and in Leicestershire to the generally wood-pasture areas in the western half of the county. By

1851 nonconformity had spread to many chalk parishes in Kent and to the lias and limestone settlements of east Leicestershire, where in almost every case it was some form of Methodism, and not the Baptist or Congregationalist faith, that took root.

In Lincolnshire, where there was very little wood-pasture but much chalk and limestone country, the Old Dissent had always been weak and Methodism by 1851 was uncommonly strongly entrenched. The same kind of development has been observed by my colleague Dr David Hey in the arable belt of magnesian limestone parishes in south Yorkshire, where Methodism flourished and Congregationalism hardly ever established itself successfully. In Northamptonshire the pattern was not so simple. This county was in some respects less sharply divided into distinct agrarian regions than Leicestershire and Kent, and the old forest areas of Rockingham and Whittlewood had in any case undergone more radical transformation than the Weald of Kent. Nevertheless, about two-thirds of the traditionally nonconformist parishes in this heartland of the Old Dissent were to be found in the woodland areas of Rockingham, Salcey and Whittlewood.

How can we explain this apparently odd association between the different branches of nonconformity and different types of rural economy? It must be stressed that the association was no more than a tendency and was not universally valid. There were no exclusively 'Methodist' or exclusively 'Baptist and Congregationalist' areas. Yet the tendency does call for some comment. One important factor was simply that the latter denominations were already well entrenched in the forest and wood-pasture areas before Methodism came into existence. Up to a point, therefore, Methodism tended to fill in the gaps left by the Old Dissent. Probably another important factor was the strongly proletarian character of some branches of Methodism, so that sects like the Primitive Methodists (and in Kent the Bible Christians) attracted many adherents in the arable regions, where farm-labourers were necessarily more numerous than in the wood-pasture districts.

It should also be noted that in some respects the gulf between Methodism and the Church of England was not so deep as that between the Old Dissent and the Establishment. As is well known the movement began within the Church and only separated from it after John Wesley's death and against his wishes. As a consequence it was sometimes able to take root in areas where the generally more independent Congregationalist and Baptist communions found no foothold. It is significant, in this context, that where dissent was able to establish itself in 'estate parishes' it was normally some form of Methodism that took root. In conclusion perhaps a word of caution is necessary. The present writer does not believe that all differences in the distribution of dissent can be explained in terms of diverse rural economies. If it were possible to examine in microscopic detail the complete social and family structure of every local and regional community, the whole tangled nexus of geological, geographical, climatic, topographical, racial, economic, cultural and religious factors in their development, it would doubtless be possible to explain some of the puzzles to which this paper affords no solution. We might then know more precisely why half the population of Lincolnshire or Bedfordshire appears to have been nonconformist in 1851 whilst only one-third of that of Kent or Westmorland comes in this category. Yet the probability remains that many peculiarities in the pattern of dissent would still elude us, for much was certainly due to purely personal or fortuitous causes. Where such matters as religious conviction are concerned, a purely deterministic explanation is out of the question. Nevertheless, although the divine fire was personal in its impetus, the way in which it spread through rural society was clearly influenced by the kind of broadly sociological influences I have been trying to describe. How far, one wonders, did these social and economic distinctions between different types of community also shape the history of education in the Victorian countryside?

Notes

1　This paper is an abridged version of part of the author's *The Pattern of Rural Dissent: the Nineteenth Century,* Department of English Local History, Occasional Papers, Second Series, No. 4 (Leicester University Press, 1972). It was originally read at the annual conference of the History of Education Society in December 1971, before *The Pattern of Rural Dissent* was published. In the limits of a conference paper much in the way of qualification and expansion had to be omitted. The third and fourth parts of *The Pattern of Rural Dissent* ('Four County Portraits' and 'Conclusion: the Genius of the Chapel Community') have been excluded, and the original footnotes have been reduced in length. For the fuller discussion of the subject the reader is referred to the Occasional Paper.

2　See Table 1.

3　A seminal article on the subject is Professor K.S. Inglis's 'Patterns of Religious Worship in 1851', *Journal of Ecclesiastical History,*

XI (1960), pp. 74-86. More recently Dr John D Gay has much to say about the distribution of dissent in *The Geography of Religion in England* (London, 1971), chapters 2, 3, 6, 7 and 8. Professor Inglis's article was concerned chiefly with urban nonconformity. Dr Gay's book does not discuss the distribution of dissent in 1851 at the *parish* level but in terms of county units. It is not possible here to discuss the general recent literature of dissent. Amongst the most important contributions have been those of Dr G.F. Nuttall (e.g., his aiticlc 'Dissenting Churches in Kent before 1700', *Journal of Ecclesiastical History*, XIV (1963).

4   It is important to note in this connection that, in the late seventeenth and early eighteenth centuries, certain rural chapels clearly acted as *regional* as well as local centres of nonconformity. This seems to have been true in Bedfordshire, Cambridgeshire, Northamptonshire, the West Country and Kent (cf. Nuttall, op. cit. p. 181 and n.), and no doubt elsewhere. The church-book of the Baptist chapel at Arnesby, Leics. (Leics. Record Office), shows that in the late seventeenth and early eighteenth centuries many members came from other villages and from places as far distant as Coventry and Ramsey (Hunts.). This was one means, of course, by which the vitality of a sect might be maintained at a time and in a district where its members formed only a very small minority of the population. It is unlikely that those members who came from far afield attended the chapel regularly, week by week. More probably they were received simply as occasional visitors, a common custom in some Victorian sects. This feature of dissent is one of great interest, but it cannot be further explored in this paper. It does not invalidate the figures given here, since these are based on the number of dissenters in *each parish,* not on the number of members of *each chapel.*

5   'Nonconformity in Country Parishes', in *Land, Church, and People: Essays presented to Professor H.P.R. Finberg (The Agricultural History Review*, XVIII, Supplement (1970)).

6   In Kent in 1672-3, for example, licences were taken out for Presbyterian meeting-houses in 32 parishes, for Baptists in 21 and for Independents in 11. See C.W. Chalklin, *Seventeenth-Century Kent: a Social and Economic History,* (London, 1965), p.227. These figures should be compared with the total of 500 non-conformist chapels in Kent recorded in the 1851 census. The typical congregation was usually smaller, moreover, in the seventeenth and early eighteenth centuries, not exceeding 40 or 50 members in many cases.

7   For a discussion of the significance, reliability and limitations of the census record see Professor K.S. Inglis's important article, 'Patterns of Religious Worship in 1851', op. cit. pp. 74-86. The value of the religious information in the census was much disputed at the time; but I accept the cogent and balanced case Professor Inglis advances (pp. 75-8), that on the whole it was

conscientiously compiled and within its limits substantially reliable. For this paper I have principally relied on the summaries and abstracts of the census given under each county and parish entry in J.M. Wilson, *The Imperial Gazetteer of England and Wales*, 6 vols (1870) (hereafter cited as *Imp. Gaz.*).

8   The attendance figures have, however, been more frequently made use of than those of chapels and 'sittings'. Briefly, the problems in utilizing the 'attendance' figures may be summarized as follows. First, Census Sunday coincided with a period of unusually severe weather, which was said to have kept many people away from church who normally attended, particularly in the northern counties: a fact that must invalidate regional comparison of attendance figures to some extent, particularly where very large parishes are concerned. Secondly, Census Sunday also coincided with a period of unusually widespread illness, again reducing the attendance below normal, in some areas apparently more than others. Thirdly, though the figures for attendants at each service on Census Sunday are given, there is no certain way of estimating the *real total* of attendants, since we do not know how many who attended in the afternoon or evening had also been present at an earlier service. It was said at the time that dissenters more often attended two or even three services than Anglicans. If this was correct (and it quite probably was) the *total* of attendants at all three services would exaggerate the real strength of dissent at the expense of the Anglican church. (Various ways of circumventing this particular problem have been suggested but none of them seems entirely satisfactory.) Fourthly, many clergy (particularly in some dioceses of the Church of England) refused to comply with the census requirement and for their churches there are no reliable attendance figures (though estimates were made by the enumerators). Finally many members of some dissenting denominations are said to have also attended services in their parish church, usually no doubt at times when there was no service in their own chapel. These will appear as Anglicans in attendance figures, of course, and there is no way of estimating their numbers.

9   In the Teesdale area of County Durham nonconformist 'sittings' were more than twice those of Anglicans. The figures were: Anglicans, 3,185; nonconformists, 6,570 (Independents, 1,065; Baptists, 540; Quakers, 333; Wesleyans, 2,619; Primitive Methodists, 1,958; Unitarians, 55). Northumberland was clearly much influenced by its proximity to Scotland, and was the only county with a considerable number of Presbyterians at this date (29,928 sittings).

10   In the St Ives area of Huntingdonshire dissenters appear to have far outnumbered Anglicans. There were more than 8,000 'sittings' in the nonconformist chapels of the area and only 5,000 in the churches of the Establishment.

11 Nuttall, op. cit. p.185, quoting from V.C.H. *Kent*, II, p. 100.
12 Dr Dennis Mills has briefly pointed out the same association in 'English Villages in the Eighteenth and Nineteenth Centuries: a Sociological Approach', *Amateur Historian*, VI (1963-5), p. 277.
13 Typologically, these freeholders' parishes often bear a close resemblance to the 'open parishes' of Warwickshire described by Dr J.M. Martin in 'The Parliamentary Enclosure Movement and Rural Society in Warwickshire', *The Agricultural History Review*, XV, i (1967), pp. 19-39. Of the fifteen places specifically mentioned as 'open parishes' by Dr Martin, at the time of enclosure, at least nine were still freeholders' settlements in 1860, and probably four others. Only two, it seems, were definitely 'estate parishes' by that date, with all their property in 'a few hands', namely Binton and Brailes.
14 Samuel Lewis, *A Topographical Dictionary of England* (1833), *sub* Lye Waste; *The National Gazetteer of Great Britain and Ireland* [1868] (hereafter cited as *Nat. Gaz.*), *sub* Lye; *Imp. Gaz.*, *sub* Lye.
15 Dr L.A. Parker, in his account of the Leicestershire hosiery industry (V.C.H. *Leics.*, III), prints (pp. 20-3) a table of villages where framework-knitting is recorded. Altogether evidence of framework-knitting occurs in 118 villages and hamlets in the eighteenth century. In many of these we do not know how many frames were involved; but Felkin's return of 1844, summarized by Dr Parker, shows that in 57 villages and towns in the county there were more than 50 stocking-frames, and in 40 there were more than 100. The latter, at any rate, must be regarded as industrial villages.
16 D.A. Iredale, *Canal Settlement: a Study of the Origin and Growth of the Canal Settlement at Barnton in Cheshire between 1775 and 1845*, Leicester Ph.D. thesis (1966), pp. 207 ff., 'Religion', and *passim*.
17 Edward Hasted, *The History and Topographical Survey of the County of Kent*, 2nd ed., V (1798), pp. 286-8; *Imp. Gaz.*, *sub* Paddock Wood; local observation.
18 V.C.H. *Kent*, III, pp. 360, 362, 364. See also the relevant entries for Ash-by-Wingham in *Imp. Gaz.* (as Ash-next-Sandwich) and *Nat. Gaz.* (as Ash-near-Sandwich); for Newington in *Imp. Gaz.* and Lewis, op. cit. Newington and Ash, it is interesting to note, both come within the category of decayed markets.
19 The following paragraphs are based on the relevant parish entries in *Imp. Gaz.* and *Nat. Gaz.* and where possible on local fieldwork in each county.
20 Others have noted a similar correlation between absentee parsons and the spread of dissent in Yorkshire, Cornwall and Devon. (Cf. R. Currie, 'A Micro-Theory of Methodist Growth', *Proceedings of the Wesley Historical Society*, XXXVI (1967), p. 69 and n.) So far as the counties under review here are concerned absenteeism,

whether of squire or parson, does not seem to have been a principal factor because, as has been mentioned, dissent was in any case far more prolific outside estate parishes altogether. Nevertheless, the effects of absenteeism may well have been significant in areas of very large estates like parts of east Leicestershire and Lindsey.

21 John Bateman, *The Great Landowners of Great Britain and Ireland* (Leicester, 1971) (reprint of 1883 ed.), pp. 224, 391, 493; *Return of Owners of Land, 1873* (1875), sections for Kent and Leicestershire.

MALCOLM SEABORNE

E. R. Robson and the Board schools of London

The name of E.R. Robson has always been associated with the buildings of the London School Board, whose first architect he was from 1871 to 1889, after which he acted as consultant architect to the Education Department in Whitehall. In his own day he acquired an international reputation as the leading expert on school architecture, and, more recently, architectural historians have pointed out the importance of his work as part of the reaction against the Gothic Revival which gained momentum in the 1870s and is generally known as the 'Queen Anne' phase of English Architecture [1]. Curiously, his work has been largely neglected by historians of education, in spite of its value from the point of view of social as well as architectural history [2].

Detailed information about Robson's career is not easy to come by. The private secretary to the chairman of the Board, who wrote an interesting account of *The Work of the London School Board* in 1900, merely remarks that Robson's 'labours in connection with school architecture are too well known to need recapitulation' [3]. The only first-hand account of his career available is that given by his son, Philip, in a memoir published at the time of his father's death in 1917; though this is relatively brief, we are fortunate in that Philip Robson was himself an architect and had worked closely with his father [4]. Philip Robson tells us that his father was born in Durham in 1835, the eldest son of Alderman Robert Robson, three times mayor of Durham. It was decided at an early stage that Edward should become an architect, and an eminently thorough apprenticeship was devised for him: three years on practical work in the building trade (to which his father belonged), three years in the offices of the well-known architect John Dobson of Newcastle upon Tyne, and three years working on church restorations in the London office of Sir George Gilbert Scott. During the year 1858

63

Robson also travelled extensively in Europe to study Continental architecture. In 1859, at the age of twenty-four, Robson went into partnership with J.W. Wilson Walton in London, but he kept a branch office in Durham, where he also held the post of architect to the Cathedral, restoring the Galilee, the Chapel of Nine Altars and the Central Tower. In 1864 Robson moved to Liverpool as architect and surveyor to the Corporation. Here his duties seem to have been mainly administrative, including property management, site acquisition, and so on. He did, however, design St Anne's Church, St Anne's Street, in red brick with Decorated tracery, and also the buildings of Stanley Park, Anfield, which Pevsner describes as 'one of the best mid-Victorian parks not only of Liverpool but of the whole North' [5]. These buildings consist of a long screen wall with Gothic details, and a number of Gothic pavilions. Indeed, up till this point, it appears that Robson's experience was almost wholly in the Gothic tradition. His versatility of outlook was, however, indicated by his design with John Weightman, the former Corporation surveyor at Liverpool, of the Municipal Offices in Dale Street, which Pevsner describes as 'in the mixed Italianate-cum-French, not stylistically definable' [6].

The circumstances of Robson's appointment to the London School Board are well documented in the Board's minutes [7]. The members of the Board, which had been set up following the Elementary Education Act of 1870, were fully apprised of the immense task which faced them in trying to bring elementary education within the reach of every child in their area, which was defined as the 114 square miles under the jurisdiction of the Metropolitan Board of Works, with a population in 1871 of over three millions. An early estimate of the number of elementary school places needed in London (after taking account of existing schools provided by the Churches) was 100,000, but this turned out to be a serious underestimate and in any event the population continued to increase rapidly, so that by 1890 the Board had provided some 400,000 school places and by 1900 over half a million [8]. The immediate need, however, was to obtain and convert buildings for temporary school purposes, and to acquire sites (which was an extremely difficult undertaking since they were most urgently needed in the heavily built up slum areas).

The Board therefore advertised for an 'architect and surveyor' at a salary of £500 p.a. This was the post for which Robson, now aged thirty-six, applied, and his experience in Liverpool must have made him a strong applicant. Six candidates were interviewed in July 1871 and four ballots were held among the members of the interviewing committee. In the first ballot, Robson obtained 17 votes, while two other candidates, William Wigginton and Thomas Porter, were eliminated. On the second ballot, John Quilter was eliminated, and on the third, Joseph James. (James was an experienced architect, who had designed the West of England Dissenters' College, now Taunton School.) On the fourth and final ballot, Robson obtained 24 votes and the remaining candidate, J.W. Morris (also an experienced school architect), five [9]. Thereafter the minutes tend to refer to Robson as the 'surveyor' and he was installed in 'the back room of the third floor' of the temporary offices of the Board, from which he operated from September 1871.

So far as new school buildings were concerned, it is clear from reading the minutes of the Works Committee of the Board that no one at that time was at all clear about what architectural form the new Board schools should take [10]. The members considered various model plans, including one submitted by the Rev. James Rigg, the principal of the Wesleyan Training College at Westminster and a member of the Board, and another suggested by Canon Cromwell, principal of the Anglican St Mark's College – for denominational rivalry still lay only just beneath the surface. There was also a strong pressure-group demanding that the design of every school should be thrown open to competition among architects on a national basis. In fact, the early schools were designed as a result of limited competitions, with usually six architects invited to submit plans – among them well-known architects like E.M. Barry, Charles Barry, Basil Champneys, George Gilbert Scott the younger and the partnership of Slater and Carpenter (who had designed the first group of Woodard schools); most of the more eminent men declined the invitation, though we shall see that Champneys was responsible for one of the earliest Board schools Robson appears in the minutes of this period as a rather shadowy figure, engaged in complex site acquisition negotiations, reporting on buildings for possible adaptation as schoolrooms, and also – significantly – drafting the conditions (including what would now be called the schedules of accommodation) for the new schools for which various outside architects were competing.

Bearing in mind Robson's earlier work in Scott's office, and then at Durham and in Liverpool, it seems likely that Robson saw himself more as a surveyor and administrator than as a designer at this stage of his career. He was however (so his son tells us) very careful to insist, when appointed to his London post, that he should be free to undertake private work while he held office. It appears that he had not been permitted to do this at Liverpool and he afterwards regretted it. In the meantime, even the limited competitions which the Board was organizing for new schools were proving to be expensive both in time and money. Architects who were successful in competitions for the design of Board schools received the usual fee of five.per cent of the contract price of the building; yet few of them could have had the expertise needed to design effectively not only the external elevations but also the relatively complex internal layouts which Robson was himself devising. In July 1872 – less than a year after he had taken up his appointment as surveyor – a committee of the Board recommended that 'a separate officer should be appointed for the acquisition of sites; [and] that Mr Robson should be appointed Architect of the Board at a salary of £1,000 per annum, with a view, amongst his other duties, to his designing and building the Schools of the Board'.[11]. This salary was a very generous one and though Robson could not of course claim any commission on the Board schools he designed, he still managed to retain the right to take on outside work. Meanwhile, he was able to afford to move with his family to a fashionable Georgian house in the Paragon, Blackheath, where he lived for the rest of his life.

During the next year or two, in spite of his heavy duties with the School Board, though no doubt with the full agreement of its members, Robson travelled to America, Switzerland, Germany, Austria, France, Belgium and Holland, 'in search' – so his son tells us – 'of the best schools'. The experience he gained by these visits abroad enabled him to formulate a distinctive rationale for the design of his new London schools, and also accounts for the considerable portion of his classic book on *School Architecture* (1874) which is taken up with a discussion of American and Continental methods. His chapters on foreign school systems certainly comprise the best short account in English (if not in any language) of the major features of these systems during this period. It is all too easy for the English historian to forget that the problems brought by mass education were not peculiar to this country. In fact, a form of the monitorial system associated in England with the names of Bell and Lancaster had been adopted in France early in the nineteenth century; somewhat later, Kay-Shuttleworth, the first secretary to the Committee of the Privy Council on Education, adopted a version of the Dutch pupil-teacher system for England; and Prussia had long been looked to as a model, especially in its provision of separate classrooms for each class of children. Within Britain itself, Stow's system in Scotland had achieved a very wide reputation and educationists were also familiar with the system of the National Education Board in Ireland. American educationists had since the 1830s been keenly interested in school developments in England and Europe (as witness the writings of such men as Alexander Bache, Horace Mann and Calvin Stowe). Later, in the 1860s especially, British educationists took close account of what was happening on the Continent: the fourth volume of the Newcastle Report on elementary education (1861), for example, was devoted to 'the state of popular education in Continental Europe', the Clarendon Report on the public schools (1864) included an 'account of the higher schools in Prussia', and the sixth volume of the Taunton Report on the endowed schools (1868) was on the subject of 'secondary education in foreign countries'. Matthew Arnold, in particular, did extensive research into education abroad and his works are referred to by Robson in his book. Robson's treatment of the educational systems in other countries therefore reminds us that there was a general growth of interest in, and writings about, school organiz- ation and architecture during the first half of the nineteenth century, beginning with such works as W.J. Adams's *The Construction and Furnishing of School-Rooms* (Boston, 1830), A Bouillon's *De la construction des maisons d'école primaire* (Paris, 1834), J.G. Hodgins's *The School House: its Architecture, External and Internal Arrangements* (Toronto, 1857) and W. Zwez's *Das Schulhaus und dessen innere Einrichtung* (Weimar, 1864). Robson may not himself have been familiar with these works, but their existence indicates that he would have found a coherent body of theory as well as practice when he visited foreign schools in the early 1870s.

It nevertheless remains true that England had been the first country to experience the effects of industrialization in its modern form, and the first in which the subject of popular education received widespread attention. The educational arrangements made for the children of the new industrial classes were, however, enormously complicated by denominational rivalry. From the beginning of the century the various religious bodies had taken considerable interest in school design, but their concern was almost wholly with the internal organization, rather than the external architectural character, of the buildings. Joseph Lancaster published his pioneer work *Hints and Directions for Building, Fitting up, and Arranging Schoolrooms on the British System of*

Education in 1811, and later the British and Foreign School Society, which popularized his methods, issued a series of *Manuals* which gave the most precise details about how the children should be arranged inside the schoolroom. The National Society, too, published a number of 'General observations on the construction and arrangement of school-rooms' in its *Annual Reports.* In the 1820s and 1830s a whole code of practice for educating children of infant age had been formulated by such writers as Samuel Wilderspin, William Wilson, James Brown and Charles Mayo, and was further elaborated in the handbooks issued by the Home and Colonial School Society. In the 1830s, too, David Stow publicized the methods he had worked out in the model schools of the Glasgow Educational Society [12]. Then in 1840 the Committee of Council on Education published a set of model plans, which were modified in 1845 and again in 1851, and in 1863 the Committee issued a set of *Rules to be Observed in Planning and Fitting-up Schools,* which were the precursors of the present-day School Building Regulations. Other manuals on school organization were also being written, especially by lecturers at some of the training colleges which had been set up after about 1840 [13].

There was, therefore, certainly no lack of material about the organization of elementary education, and the chapters on this subject in Robson's book on *School Architecture,* though derivative, provide a useful summary of these developments. The difficulty in fact was that there were too many systems and, although the official *Rules* were beginning to bring about greater uniformity, there was still a real need to decide on what seemed to be the one best system for London and to apply it consistently. The great contribution of Robson and the London School Board was to devise a system in many respects in advance of that laid down by the Government Education Department. Once the London Board had shown the way, other Boards, particularly in the large towns, followed suit.

The way that London acted as a pacemaker for the rest of the country may be illustrated with reference to the basic question of how the children should be arranged inside the school. The standard arrangement laid down in the official *Rules* provided for a large schoolroom with a smaller classroom associated with it; inside the schoolroom, the children were to be arranged in groups of long parallel desks set out in three rows, with the groups separated from each other by curtains and taken by pupil-teachers under the supervision of the headmaster. The London School Board modified this arrangement by increasing the

Fig. 1. London Board School. A double classroom showing dual arrangement of desks.

number of classrooms and by introducing dual desks set out in five rows from the front to the back of the class (see Fig. 1) [14]. Robson clearly saw that, bearing in mind the large amount of expository teaching which was usual in the schools by this date, the limit to the size of a classroom was the range of the teacher's voice. He further realized that, given the existing pupil-teacher system and the relative scarcity of fully qualified adult teachers, it was not yet possible to abandon the large schoolroom entirely and to adopt the full Prussian system of arranging each class in a separate classroom, since the headmaster still needed to keep personal control of the whole school. Robson also appreciated the value of the large schoolroom as a place of general assembly and notes with interest the 'examination halls' in the German schools. He points out, however, that these were used on relatively few occasions, and (while in general agreeing about the excellence of the Prussian schools) he makes a number of reservations about them, including the over-large size of classes, the inadequate sanitary arrangements and the absence of women teachers. Very early in its history the London School Board experimented with a school

Fig. 2. Jonson Street School, Stepney. (Architect T.R. Smith.)

built on the 'Prussian plan' (this was the Jonson Street School in Stepney, designed by T. Roger Smith, illustrated in Fig. 2). Robson's conclusion that there were insufficient adult teachers to make this plan suitable for general adoption was correct for that date, though eventually the London School Board managed to persuade the Education Department to pay extra grants for a central hall as well as separate classrooms to be built in every new school, a policy followed after 1891 in London and many other large towns [15].

How far can it be claimed that Robson was also an innovator in the architectural style chosen for the new Board schools? He was by no means the first English architect to interest himself in school design; and, in particular, Henry Kendall, whose father helped to found the Institute of British Architects, had earlier made an eloquent plea for the employment of professional architects for elementary schools in his book *Designs for Schools and Schoolhouses* published in 1847. Kendall urged the introduction of Gothic forms into school architecture and many of the National schools built in the 1850s and 60s were designed by well-known Gothicists. Another influential work was *Schools and School Houses* (1852) by Joseph Clarke, who was a founder of the Architectural Museum. The most systematic previous treatment of the subject, however, was the book on *School Architecture* published in 1848 by Henry Barnard, who was secretary of the Board of Commissioners of Common Schools in Connecticut. Even allowing, however, for the fact that Barnard's work was written with reference mainly to American conditions, it is also important to note that he was an educationist and not an architect, so that his book, like the many manuals of the time, was little concerned with the external architectural style chosen for schools. Kendall and Clarke, on the other hand, were architects but not educationists and they showed themselves only marginally concerned with matters of internal school organization. Robson's great achievement was to make himself proficient in both the architectural and educational aspects of school design and to integrate the two. His work for the London School Board also marks a very important stage between the pre-1870 system under which school architects worked as individuals dealing with private clients, and the post 1902 system under which architects employed by local and central government authorities were mainly responsible for further developments in school design. Robson was the archetype of the new civic official, more than comparable with Herr Raschdoff, town architect of Cologne, whom Robson mentions in his book, and Félix

Narjoux, the town architect of Paris, who later in the 1870s wrote a number of works on similar lines to Robson's. It is significant, however, that the standard works on English school architecture after 1902 were written by the chief architect at the Board of Education [16].

No claim has, of course, ever been advanced that Robson originated the so-called 'Queen Anne' style: the question which needs to be explored is how he came to adopt and develop it for the Board schools of London. The origin of the style has been detected in such buildings as Nesfield's lodge at Kew Gardens, built in 1867, and a number of houses designed by Norman Shaw soon afterwards, though other architectural historians point out the importance of the earlier work of John Shaw, who built the Royal Naval School (now Goldsmiths' College) at Deptford in 1843 and Wellington College in Berkshire, which was completed in 1859 in a style which has many features later called 'Queen Anne' [17]. There is general agreement that this style grew in popularity in the early 1870s as a reaction against the prevalent Gothic, but few writers agree about its essential characteristics, except that it usually owed little to the original style of the reign of Queen Anne. It has most recently been described as 'a kind of architectural cocktail, with a little genuine Queen Anne in it, a little Dutch, a little Flemish, a touch of Robert Adam and a dash of Francois 1er' [18]. Perhaps the most useful label is the 'brick and sash' style, in contrast, that is to say, with the stone walls and mullioned windows of the Victorian Gothic style which had until then predominated. Robson himself considered that 'the only really simple brick style available as a foundation is that of the time of the Jameses, Queen Anne, and the early Georges' (*School Architecture*, p. 323) and, like most of the other exponents of the new style, he argued that it was chiefly a revival of older vernacular traditions of building (ibid. p.306). Certainly this vernacular element is present, especially among those architects sympathetic to the so-called 'aesthetic movement' of this period – and here it may be noted that Robson (so his son tells us) possessed furniture designed by Philip Webb, glass made by Morris and Burne-Jones, and a gold watch designed by Dante Gabriel Rossetti. Though it is difficult to generalize about the architectural detail of the 'Queen Anne' style, historians agree that it expressed a new and less earnest spirit among the Victorian middle classes, who were growing tired of the gloomy inconvenience of the private houses built by the Gothicists.

As for the new Board schools, Robson's partner in private practice for a few years after he was appointed to the London School Board was

J.J. Stevenson, whose 'Red House' built in Bayswater Road in 1871 is usually included as an early example of the 'Queen Anne' style. In his book on *House Architecture* Stevenson says of the London Board schools that 'for the architecture of a few of the earliest of these I am responsible, having found by the practical experience of a house I built for myself in this manner, that the ["Queen Anne"] style adapts itself to every modern necessity and convenience' [19]. Philip Robson, however, says that his father told him that 'he was occupied often in the afternoons rubbing out what John [Stevenson] had done in the morning'. The relationship between Robson and Stevenson remains somewhat obscure, but in any event the new style was being widely publicized at this period: Norman Shaw was building Lowther Lodge and New Zealand Chambers just at the time when the new Board

Fig. 3. Harwood Road School. (Architect B. Champneys.)

schools were being planned, and one of the earliest schools built for the London Board by Basil Champneys in Harwood Road, Fulham (illustrated in Fig. 3), was in a version of this style. There were in fact compelling reasons for adopting a new style for the London Board schools. In the first place, as Robson was quick to realize, the Gothic style of school building was associated with the religious societies and denominational rivalry. Nonconformists in the earlier part of Victoria's reign had rarely chosen Gothic for their schools: at Sheffield, Liverpool and Leicester, for example, the important nonconformist proprietary schools were in versions of the Palladian style, which was chosen in conscious reaction against the Tudor Gothic of the Anglican proprietary schools in the same towns. In the fifties and sixties it is true that Gothic invaded school architecture on an extensive scale, though the Free Churches tended to prefer the so-called 'Elizabethan' or some version of the 'Italianate' style for their schools (a notable surviving example is the school built by Sir Titus Salt at Saltaire near Shipley in 1868). In this way the growing taste for external ornamentation could be satisfied without necessarily resorting to Gothic. The new School Board of London was dominated by members of the Progressive or Liberal party and Robson rightly assessed their desire to establish a new secular and civic style for their schools in contrast to the Gothic style with its ecclesiastical associations. Even so, it may be noted that Robson was no fanatic in adopting versions of the 'Queen Anne' style for his schools – indeed, some of his early schools, as, for example, that illustrated in Fig. 4, included elements of Gothic. (A similar transition from forms of Gothic to more secular styles may be seen in other areas where the school board was controlled by the Liberals, as at Leicester.)

Secondly, one has to consider the effect on school building of the very restricted sites available, which would have forced any architect to design tall buildings. This was no new phenomenon in London, where elementary schools of several storeys had been built well before 1870, an interesting surviving example being E.M. Barry's Gothic school in Endell Street, off Shaftesbury Avenue, which was built in 1860 with five floors to accommodate no less than 1,500 children [20]. There is no doubt, however, that the coming of universal compulsory education made the building of large schools a necessity, especially in London. Similarly, the need for economy – and the constant attacks on the London Board for its alleged extravagance – dictated that brick should be the main material used. As for the inside of the buildings, it was

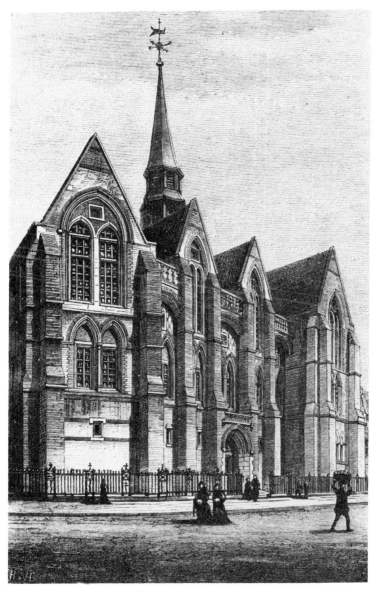

Fig. 4. Mansfield Place School. (Architect E.R. Robson.)

essential to build high rooms to provide sufficient light and ventilation for the very large number of (often dirty) children who had to be accommodated; so too, the inevitably hard wear which the buildings received obliged Robson to think in terms of glazed brick and other hard surfaces for the interior finishes. For the exteriors of his schools, however, it is much to Robson's credit that he chose light yellow stock brick, with red brick used only for dressings (see, for example, Fig. 5). He also avoided terracotta, relying instead for external ornament on gracefully carved title panels and cartouches cut in the brick or stone and showing floral patterns and figured bas-reliefs. Though industrial pollution, subsequent additions to the buildings and major changes in their surroundings (such as road works and vast new housing schemes) have marred many of Robson's schools, those which survive more rarely have the grim and stark appearance so usual with the red brick and terracotta buildings put up by school boards in other towns, often in direct imitation of the London schools.

However much Robson may have owed to other architects, or had dictated to him by the circumstances of the time, the fact nevertheless remains that he did have the foresight to see the potentiality of the 'Queen Anne' style and to adapt — rather than merely adopt — it for his schools. Indeed, one architectural historian goes so far as to suggest that, instead of the 'Queen Anne' style, we should call it the 'Board School' style [21]. A point which needs to be stressed, however, is that the 'Queen Anne' style began as a revolution in the building of private houses for the middle and upper classes, often on pleasant rural or suburban sites, and it was the domestic and 'picturesque' character of these houses which chiefly attracted contemporaries. It is very doubtful whether, in building large schools for the working classes in the mainly industrialized parts of London, Robson could ever have hoped to imitate the 'Queen Anne' style as it had originally been conceived. His schools had to exemplify the civic pride of the new School Board of London, and also the new enlightenment brought to the common people by the Elementary Education Act of 1870 — for Sherlock Holmes in *The Naval Treaty* was not alone in seeing the new Board schools as 'big, isolated clumps of buildings rising above the slates, like brick islands in a lead-coloured sea . . . out of which will spring the wiser, better England of the future'. Although Robson claimed, perhaps rightly, that stock brick was the local vernacular building material for London, his designs drew on motifs from various parts of this country and abroad (the stepped gables shown in Fig. 6 are, for example,

Fig. 5. Wornington Road School. (Architect E.R. Robson.)

common on buildings in East Anglia and in Scotland and are said to have been introduced from Holland in the fifteenth century) [22]. Probably this does not matter. But it is surely overstating the case to suggest, as one writer recently has, that 'Robson's approach marked a conscious acceptance of the genius loci of London' [23]. Robson's own roots were in the North, and the school building programme which he supervised was so large that he was often unable to visit his sites until the jobs were completed: inevitably there was delegation and standardization, though his buildings certainly showed more variety of treatment than became usual with later schools. The same writer is much nearer the truth in praising Robson for 'the superb confidence and virility with which he and his staff carried through the development of this style, giving power and sometimes grandeur where its originators could only achieve charm' [24].

Confidence and drive characterized Robson's whole personality, and he also seems to have been completely in sympathy with the educational advances of the post-1870 period. Early in his book on *School Architecture* he refers to the 'popular boon' of universal elementary education and, although his name is more usually associated with the Board schools, it is worth noting that he also had advanced views on the subject of secondary education, as evidenced in his chapter on 'Middle Schools', where he criticizes the older public schools whose endowments 'often intended for the meritorious youth of humble rank, have fallen into the lap of others better able to pay'. He also commends the work of the Endowed Schools Commissioners, mentions the inadequacy of the existing schools for girls and concludes by pointing to the need for 'the establishment of a complete national system' of secondary education. Here he is speaking not simply as an architect, but as an educational reformer.

His remarkable energy is also shown by the number of other buildings he designed as a private architect, including several important secondary schools [25]. He was responsible for the Girls' High schools at Blackheath and at Truro, and for extensions to Cheltenham Ladies' College, as well as for Wilson's Grammar School, Camberwell, Ashton Grammar School, Dunstable, and — in the adult education sphere — the People's Palace in Mile End Road, London (now Queen Mary College), and Firth College in Sheffield. His son boasted of the occasion when he converted a market hall into a picture gallery in six weeks (the New Gallery, Regent Street), and how in 1904-5 he rebuilt the Jews' Free School in Spitalfields (reputed to be the largest element-

Fig. 6. Winstanley Road School. (Architect E.R. Robson.)

ary school in the world, with 3,500 children, 4 halls and 76 classrooms) without teaching having to be stopped for a single day. Contemporary photographs of Robson show a formidable, almost Bismarckian figure [26], though his son states that he had a 'pungent wit' and a large circle of friends. He grew impatient of the bureaucratic methods of the Board of Education which replaced the former Government departments concerned with education in 1899 and soon afterwards retired from official work. He died at Blackheath in 1917, aged eighty-one. His pioneer work on *School Architecture* remains as a valuable source of information about the development of school architecture in the nineteenth century both in England and abroad; and there are many touches in it which reveal something of the powerful character which underlies it. But his true monument may be said to survive in the Board schools which still raise their heads above the mean houses of the less frequented parts of London.

Notes

1   I am much indebted to Dr J. Mordaunt Crook for advice on the sources of the 'Queen Anne' phase of architecture, and for the interest he has shown in my own researches.
2   E.R. Robson's book on *School Architecture* (1874) has been reprinted by Leicester University Press in its Victorian Library series (1972). This chapter is based on the new introduction written for it by the author of the present essay.
3   T.A. Spalding, *The Work of the London School Board,* 2nd ed. (London, 1900), p. 68, n. 3.
4   P.A. Robson's memoir was published in the *Journal of the Royal Institute of British Architects* (February 1917), pp. 92-6. See also the report of a joint paper by E.R. and P.A. Robson on educational buildings, read to the Congress of the Royal Institute of Public Health, in *The Builder* (29 July 1905). P.A. Robson also wrote a book on *School Planning* (London, 1911).
5   N. Pevsner, *South Lancashire* (Harmondsworth, 1969), p.212. St Anne's Church is described on p. 205. (This church was demolished in 1971.)
6   Ibid. p.161.
7   These are preserved in the Greater London Council Record Office in County Hall, Westminster.
8   S. Maclure, *One Hundred Years of London Education 1870-1970* (London, 1970), pp. 27-8.
9   Minutes of the School Board for London, Vol. II, p. 409.
10   School Board for London. Works Minute Books, January 1871-April 1872 (ref. 927A) and April-October 1872 (ref. 927B), *passim.*
11   Works Minutes, Vol. II, p. 132.

12 D. Stow, *The Training System* (1836), which went to an 11th edition in 1859.
13 The development of elementary school plans and internal organization is traced in detail in M. Seaborne, *The English School: its Architecture and Organization 1370-1870* (London, 1971), Chs. 8 and 10.
14 All the illustrations shown here are from Robson's book on *School Architecture* (1874).
15 The planning of the London Board schools after 1874 is described in Spalding, op. cit. pp. 59-73, and in the *Final Report of the School Board for London 1870-1904,* 2nd ed. (1904), pp. 34-77.
16 F. Clay, *Modern School Building*, 1st ed. (London, 1902), 2nd ed. (expanded, 1906), and 3rd ed. (rewritten, 1929).
17 See N. Pevsner, *Berkshire* (Harmondsworth, 1966), pp. 260-2, and Seaborne, op. cit. pp.255-6 and pls. 215-16.
18 M. Girouard in *The Listener* (22 April 1971), p. 504.
19 J.J. Stevenson, *House Architecture* (1880), Vol. 1, p. 348.
20 Seaborne, op. cit. pp. 223-4, and pl. 184.
21 H.S. Goodhart-Rendel, *English Architecture Since the Regency* (London, 1953), p. 163.
22 'Crow-step' gables are illustrated in J. Harris and J. Lever, *Illustrated Glossary of Architecture 850-1830* (London, 1966), pl. 125, and in A. Clifton-Taylor, *The Pattern of English Building*, 2nd ed. (London, 1965), pls. 210c and 245a. See also T.D. Atkinson, *A Glossary of Terms Used in English Architecture*, 6th ed. (London, 1946), pp. 77-8.
23 D. Gregory-Jones, 'Towers of Learning', *The Architectural Review* (June 1958), p. 395.
24 Ibid. p.398.
25 There are lists of buildings designed by E.R. Robson in *The Builder* (2 February 1917) and at the end of P.A. Robson's memoir in the *Journal of the Royal Institute of British Architects* (February 1917). There is also a very useful typed list, with references, in the R.I.B.A. Library, dated August 1958.
26 Photographs of E.R. Robson, with brief accounts of his work, were published in *The Building News* (5 September 1890), and in *The Builders' Journal* (28 May 1895).

JOHN LAWSON

The use of ecclesiastical records for the history of education

Local studies in the history of education may be said to serve two rather different but related ends. One is simply to examine the development of particular institutions or educational conditions in particular local communities mainly or entirely as an end in itself and for its own sake. Recent examples include the essays on Leicestershire education from 1540 to 1940 edited by Professor Simon, and Dr Wardle's study of education in nineteenth-century Nottingham. The lists of theses published in the Society's *Bulletin* show how much work of this kind is currently being done. A second object of the local approach may be the systematic accumulation of evidence in given areas in order to enlarge or verify or revise what is known or assumed about education generally at any period of time. Professor Jordan's demonstration of the importance of private charity in expanding educational opportunity in Tudor and early Stuart England was based on accumulated local examples. Accepted notions about post-Restoration education and the influence of the S.P.C.K. in the early eighteenth century have been queried by Joan Simon's examination of the Leicestershire evidence. Malcolm Seaborne's book on English school architecture is based, and only could be based, on particular, i.e. local, examples.

For any local study the record sources and materials may be of either local or national provenance. Education has always been predominantly a local enterprise and therefore most of the evidence for it, certainly before the nineteenth century, is likely to have been produced locally and still to exist locally. Only when education becomes a Government concern in the nineteenth century do central records about it proliferate. For this reason there is little specifically about education among the records of the State before the nineteenth century, and what there is resulted from local inquiries. The earliest example is perhaps the collection of chantry certificates returned to the Court of Augmentations by commissioners appointed in each county under the Chantry Acts of 1545 and 1547, the school continuation warrants that followed, the annual payments of Crown stipends to successive masters of former chantry schools recorded in the receivers' accounts, and the returns of the special Exchequer commissions later appointed to report on the conduct of these schools. All these are in the Public Record Office.

Other relatively early State records, also originating in local inquiries, are the proceedings of the Commissioners for Charitable Uses appointed under Acts of 1598 and 1601 to investigate alleged abuses of charities, including schools, and to rectify them by Chancery decree. The Commonwealth produced more Government records bearing on education (chiefly school trusts and grants to schoolmasters) and some of these have found their way into the British Museum and the Lambeth Library. Two national collections of private documents which are of local concern are the Wase papers of the 1670s in the Bodleian and the correspondence files of the S.P.C.K. All these are well known and I mention them only as exceptions to the general rule that until the nineteenth century the main sources of educational history, in its institutional and social aspects, are to be found locally.

Of these sources, the most important and the most neglected are the records of the Church [1]. Education for most of its history was regarded as essentially a religious or moral activity; its surveillance was the Church's responsibility, exercised through the administrative and judicial system which the Church developed. The records which this system produced at the diocesan no less than at the parochial level were local in that they were concerned to a large extent with particular people in particular places. None of them however deals exclusively with education until the nineteenth century. They are concerned with other matters and provide information about education incidentally, even accidentally.

This is no less true of secular records, of course. Almost any kind, however unlikely, may throw unexpected light on education. At an inquisition held at York in 1297 to prove the full age of the heir to an estate at Whiston near Rotherham, one Jolland de Newton, 'aged 40 or more', deposed that the heir was born in 1276, a date he remembered because he had come home to Whiston for the Christmas holiday from Lincoln school, and also because his own son was born at the same time [2]. Here, quite by chance, we have evidence for a school at

Lincoln in 1276 attended by a man of nineteen or more who was presumably married, confirming other evidence that medieval grammar schools were not for boys only, but for men of any age who wanted to learn grammar, and not necessarily to become priests.

In view of their bulk and importance, the records which the Church accumulated over the centuries have been remarkably little explored by historians of education. Perhaps there are two main reasons for this neglect. One is the confused state, until recently, of many diocesan registries, their resources stored in dust-laden cardboard boxes and brown-paper parcels, largely unlisted and unindexed. Another is the technical difficulties posed by many of the documents themselves – the Latin, the palaeography, the legal forms. For these reasons, the corpus of edited material in print, translated or simply transcribed, especially for the pre-Reformation period, has grown very little since the pioneering work of A.F. Leach about the turn of the last century. An assistant charity commissioner by profession, Leach was also one of a generation of Latin-bred scholars who read their manuscript Latin charters and registers almost as easily as they read *The Times*. As expertise of this kind becomes rarer, exploitation of medieval manuscript sources for the history of education will perforce have to be left to professional medievalists who choose to work in this field.

The most important ecclesiastical records are those produced by the bishop in his diocese, and since the last war many of these have been transferred to county record offices or other repositories. The York diocesan archives, for instance, are now housed in the Borthwick Institute of Historical Research. Of medieval records the chief are the bishops' registers and a slowly increasing number of those that survive are being made available in print [3]. The register records the official acts of the bishop's reign: ordinations, inductions, dispensations, visitations and such other items as he or his registrar thought fit to preserve, often with little coherence or system. Medieval registers throw incidental light on the education of the time. They suggest that in dioceses with a monastic cathedral the bishop himself licensed schoolmasters, whilst in dioceses with a secular cathedral the chancellor ordinarily had this responsibility, although there were many exceptions. They provide some evidence for the educational standards of the parish clergy, candidates for ordination or induction sometimes being rejected for their 'literary insufficiency' or accepted on condition of further study in the schools. Other clergy, usually well-beneficed rectors, are given leave of absence from their livings in order to study. Visitation records reveal something of the educational activity of monks and nuns. There may be entries concerning the education of the bishop's nephews or wards. Archbishop Giffard in 1276 at his manor of Bishop Burton near Beverley instructed his bailiff to pay the fees and expenses of a ward and two companions at Beverley school [4]. Archbishop Greenfield's register shows him arranging for his Italian bankers to remit allowances to his nephew and another scholar (perhaps his private tutor) at the University of Paris including the expenses of his nephew's 'inception' in 1310 [5]. In rare instances the statutes of a new school were copied into the bishop's register as a safe place of record. Those of the chantry school at Wotton under Edge, Gloucestershire (1384), are in the register of Bishop Wakefield of Worcester [6]. Those of the chantry school at Newland, Gloucestershire (1446), are in that of Bishop Spofford of Hereford (and two subsequent revisions in Bishop Stanbury's) [7]. Those of East Retford, Nottinghamshire (1552), are in Archbishop Holgate's at York [8]. Why some were so recorded and not others is by no means clear.

Less explored than the bishop's registers are the records of deans and chapters. Here one would expect to find evidence about the grammar schools which the canon law required cathedrals and similar collegiate churches to maintain. These schools were the responsibility of the chapter's chancellor, who nominated and licensed the school-master and allowed others in the city or the diocese at his discretion. The one surviving act book of the chapter of Beverley minster was edited by A.F. Leach [9]. The first entry dates from 1286, the last from 1347, the majority fall between 1302 and 1340. Among the diverse items of chapter business here recorded are many relating to the chapter's grammar school. They are well known from their inclusion in Leach's *Early Yorkshire Schools*, and they make this one of the best documented schools of this period.

The school's standing is indicated by the fact that all five successive masters mentioned in the act book are styled *magister*, and we may assume that at this period this means they were all full graduates who had completed their necessary regency at Oxford or Cambridge [10]. Moreover, one of the school's customs was for the master to create 'bachelors'; these were probably older pupils, priests or deacons on the minster's staff, whom he appointed to assist him in the school after suitable tests of proficiency, in much the same way as regent masters admitted their own bachelors in the university schools after 'determination' [11]. The master was nominated by the chancellor for a term of three years (as was usual at York during this period) and he ruled the school as the chancellor's deputy. The monopoly of grammar teaching within the liberty of the minster which his appointment conferred was protected by the chancellor against the competition of unlicensed rivals, ultimately even by excommunication [12]. In none of the act book references to the schoolmaster is his exact status in the hierarchy made clear, except that at this period he was expected to be a priest and did reading and singing duty in the choir, but was not one of the canons.

The appointment of a new master in 1306 is recorded with remarkable fullness [13]. On this occasion, perhaps in order to redact what had previously been only unwritten custom, the documents produced at each stage of the process were carefully copied into the act book as a permanent record. On 30 September the chancellor, Master Robert de Bitham, appears personally before the chapter's auditor of causes in the chapter house and presents to him Master Roger de Bolton to rule the grammar school for three years, the school then being vacant and in the chancellor's gift. When the chancellor has read out the formal instrument of collation he presents it duly sealed to the new master. The latter then submits what must surely be the earliest recorded example of a written testimonial for a school post. It was granted him at Cambridge on the previous 2 July in the full congregation of regents by the vice chancellor, Master Richard de Aston (the chancellor then being absent) and presumably it was given expressly for this appointment, since it is addressed to the chapter (or some similar body) as *vestra universitas reverenda*. It witnesses that Master Roger de Bolton had diligently studied the liberal arts, as his performance in the public exercises had shown, that he had served his regency and behaved himself well and continued his studies in moral philosophy, thus richly deserving the praise of honourable men. This having been read out, the auditor admits the chancellor's nominee as suitable to teach the school; he administers the oath of obedience to the chapter and its officers and the new master pledges himself to teach the school faithfully and to observe all the customs of the school and church of Beverley. Finally, he is put into physical possession of the schoolhouse by the master of works, 'as the custom of our church demands and requires'. Here in one single act book we have a whole area of medieval education illuminated. Pre-Reformation chapter act books survive at all the secular cathedrals, the earliest at York (1290), Lincoln (1305), Salisbury (1329) and Exeter (1382) and at Southwell and Ripon as well as Beverley.

Wills are an important category of ecclesiastical records of local provenance which sometimes shed light on education. All wills had to be proved in a church court until 1858 – in the archdeacon's court, or (if the estate was in more than one archdeaconry) in the bishop's consistory court, or (if the estate was in more than one diocese) in the prerogative court of either Canterbury or York. The court records consist of the original wills bearing the testator's and witnesses' signatures or marks, and copies written up in the registers. During the past twenty years or so many have been transferred to county record offices or other repositories, such as the Borthwick Institute at York. Some have been transcribed, others indexed, by county record societies. The vast majority are still unexplored [14].

The value of wills as a source for educational and other social history was clearly shown by Professor Jordan – they provided his main evidence for the massive endowment of education by private philanthropy between about 1560 and 1640 [15]. From the fifteenth century, wills may reveal otherwise unknown schoolmasters, as testators, executors, witnesses, or simply by chance mention. A Scarborough burgess in 1457 asks to be buried in the parish church 'near the font, where Hugo Rasen, formerly grammar school master, was buried' [16]. In 1465 a burgess of Hedon near Hull bequeaths all his grammar books to the chapel of St Augustine for the use of the grammar school there, thus confirming the existence of a school in the church [17]. Wills suggest that it was by no means unusual for pre-Reformation schoolmasters to be married and therefore not priests. Bequests for the support of sons or nephews at school or the university or one of the Inns of Court or Chancery indicate the clientele of these institutions, the age range, the usual period of study and the expense. In 1391 a York merchant leaves 20 marks to find his son at the university for four years – the length of the B.A. course – at five marks a year [18]. A Beverley tradesman in 1444 leaves the rents of a house in Hull to maintain a nephew at school until he is sixteen [19]. A Nottingham man directs in 1529 that his son

> shalbe put to lerne, unto such tyme that he be xv yeres olde, and to be put to some good scole, and he to have every yere to his exhibicion fyve marc; and, after that, to be putto Oxford or to Cambridge, to he com to the age of xx^{ti} yeres, every yere having fyve poundes. And after he be xxth, to be put to the Innes of Courte, to he come to the age of xxiiijth; and he to have every yere tenne marc. [20].

Wills provide some indirect evidence about educational standards. Clergy often bequeath books to individuals, sometimes with a reversion on their death to a church or college library. Laymen also are increasingly revealed by their wills as book owners, as literacy in English spread in the fifteenth century. Writing too had by then ceased to be merely a technical, professional skill — the Earl of Northumberland making his will in English in 1485 specifically tells us that he is writing it with his own hand, as does a Hull merchant in 1487 [21].

From the Reformation and especially from the seventeenth century the ecclesiastical records that have survived increase in bulk. Latin comes to be used together with English in mongrel fashion, then is retained only for the legal forms of documents, finally giving way to English during the eighteenth century. But if language and handwriting present fewer problems, difficulties still remain in the largely unparticularized contents of some of the archives, though this is changing with the great improvements in their custody made over the past twenty years or so. When these records have all been sorted, calendared and indexed we shall have a vast new quarry of source material which will add considerably to our knowledge of education at this time [22].

The main ecclesiastical records bearing on education during this period are those that resulted from the responsibility for supervising schoolmasters and what they taught which, in the cause of religious uniformity after the establishment of the Church of England, the bishops were given by royal injunctions and canon law, and ultimately by Act of Parliament. These are the records arising from the episcopal licensing of schoolmasters and from visitation. It is from these that much of the evidence comes for the existence of private schools, many perhaps otherwise unknown, as distinct from the public endowed schools.

'That no man shall take upon him to teach, but such as shall be allowed by the ordinary' was one of the Queen's injunctions in 1559. This was made part of the law of the Church of England by the canons of 1571 and 1604 and reinforced by statute in 1604 and 1662. To obtain the bishop's licence the applicant after 1604 was required by canon law to subscribe to the royal supremacy, the Book of Common Prayer and the Thirty-Nine Articles. The records that licensing produced are fullest for the decades following the Uniformity Act of 1662, but then as earlier there are deficiencies and inconsistencies that defy explanation. Every diocese must have accumulated documents connected with licensing but they have attracted little attention from

historians of education. The Norwich subscription books were made
the subject of an analtyical study in 1937 [23], but these appear to be
the only one, though subscription books have been used alongside
other evidence in regional studies, those of the Archdeaconry of
Leicester by Joan Simon, for example.

When a man went to obtain the licence to teach in some particular
school or place, he would take with him nomination papers from the
school trustees or letters testimonial from the parson and church-
wardens or other influential inhabitants. At York, most of these that
survive are of post-Restoration date.

On 13 January 1676 the corporation of Hull confirmed the election
of Robert Pell as master of the town grammar school and furnished him
with a letter of nomination addressed to the Archbishop of York as
diocesan:

> Since the death of Mr John Parks our late School Master upon the
> testimony of some worthy ministers and gentlemen of note of the
> sobriety and accurate abilities in learning of the bearer Mr Robert
> Pell Wee have according to our Charter nominated elected and
> chosen the said Mr Pell to be Mr of our Grammar Schoole. Wee
> pray yor Graces approbation thereof may be added by granting him
> yor licence to teach the same school as Master . . . [24].

The nomination papers or testimonial letters having been presented, the
applicant made his subscription in a paper book according to a common
form which he himself or the clerk copied out for signature:

> I, Robert Pell, litteratus, now to be admitted Mr of the free school
> of Kingston upon Hull in the County & Diocese of York do willingly
> & ex animo subscribe to the preceding declaration & all things
> therein contained this sixteenth day of January 1676.
>
> Rob. Pell [25]

The same books served for schoolmasters and clergy and all others who
subscribed for a licence; there were none for schoolmasters separately.
Copies of the actual licence bearing the bishop's seal were not kept by
the registry, but the nomination papers might be endorsed to the effect
that a licence had been issued (*emanavit licentia*) or a note of the fact
made in the Institution Books:

> Licentia ad docendum et erudiendum pueros et adolescentulos in
> libera schola de Kingston super Hull . . . concessa Roberto Pell literato
> 16o die Januarii 1676. [26]

On the same day that Pell subscribed at the diocesan registry in
York, he also appeared before Archbishop Richard Sterne at his palace

at Bishopthorpe to make the declaration required by Section VII of the
Act of Uniformity of 1662, the Archbishop himself witnessing this
subscription (perhaps because he stood in a special relationship to the
school at Hull, the Corporation's nominee having to receive the
Archbishop's formal approval, according to the town's charter):

> I, Robert Pell, literate, now to be admitted Master of the ffree
> schoole of Kingston super Hull in the County and Diocese of York
> Doe declare, That it is not lawfull upon any pretence whatsoever to
> take armes against the king; and that I do abor that Trayterous
> Position of taking Armes by his Authority against his Person or
> against those that are commissionated by him.
> And that I will conform to the Liturgy of the Church of England as
> it is now by Law established
> And I do Declare, that I do hold there lyth no Obligation upon me,
> or any other Person from the Oath, commonly called The Solemne
> League & Covenant,, to endeavour any Change or Alteration of
> Government, either in Church or State, And that the same was in
> itself an unlawfull oath, Imposed upon the Subjects of this Realm
> against the known Laws and Liberties of this Kingdome.
>
>   Robt Pell.
>
> This Declaration and Acknowledgement was Subscribed by the
> above named Robt Pell Schoolemaster of Kingston upon Hull
> in the Diocese of York before me. Witness my hand & seal the
> sixteenth day of January 16$\frac{6}{7}$ Rich. Ebor.

The Archbishop's licence under his seal and signature was then
presented to Pell. On his return to Hull both the declaration and the
licence were copied into the Corporation's Bench Book as a permanent
record [27]. Because of the comparative rarity of schoolmasters'
licences, this example is printed below as an appendix (see p. 96).

In the subscription books are to be found teachers of all kinds,
non-graduates teaching ABC, petty and English schools, graduates —
both clergy and laymen — teaching grammar schools, public or private,
in towns and villages; but seldom any women. Although the need for
the licence was not abolished until 1869, it was increasingly disregarded
and became almost optional in the eighteenth century. Nevertheless,
the records concerning it remain a valuable source. Nomination papers
and subscriptions supply the names of at least fifteen successive schoolmasters in the East Riding village of Nafferton between 1710 and
1790 [28].

Visitation was a formal inspection carried out by the bishop or
archdeacon in the cause of ecclesiastical discipline. The bishop held his
primary visitation within a year of his translation and thereafter

ordinary visitations at three or more yearly intervals. The archdeacon was supposed to visit annually. In preparation for these, citations were sent to each parish calling on incumbents, churchwardens, parish clerks and schoolmasters (and also surgeons and midwives, who likewise had to be licensed) to appear at a stated time and place to meet the visitor. Visitation articles were also issued, asking the incumbent and church-wardens for information on specific points. One or more of these invariably enquired about teachers in the parish — whether they were licensed or not, if they were of good character, regularly attended church with their scholars and taught them the catechism [29]. In the eighteenth century written answers to these articles were required on printed forms. On the appointed day those who had been called appeared before the visitor and his registrar; the presentments or written replies were handed in; clergy exhibited their ordination and institution papers, preachers, surgeons, midwives and schoolmasters their licences. Some time later, injunctions were sent to incumbents ordering the correction of faults which had been revealed by the presentments and by answers to the visitor's oral questions (*detecta*) and then set out in his findings (*comperta*). Disciplinary proceedings subsequently taken against offenders (including absentee or unlicensed schoolmasters) were reported in the act books and other records of the bishop's or archdeacon's court [30].

The earliest Court Book at York dates from 1561 and it contains details of the examinations in 1563 and 1564, presumably after visitation, of some 57 named schoolmasters from all parts of the diocese, giving assessments of their academic competence, and a copy of the articles of religion on which they were examined and to which they subscribed [31]. Why these, and not others, were examined is obscure. There is only one from York, none from Hull, but four from Beverley. Both the master and the usher of the grammar schools at Malton and Pocklington were examined. Of eighteen schoolmasters from the East Riding, most were from small villages and seven of them were also incumbents or curates. At Scarborough the schoolmaster was the vicar. From his examination we learn that he had studied for four years at Corpus Christi College, Cambridge, and been assistant to the regius professor of Hebrew, that he was found to be a capable and proper person, expert in both Hebrew and especially Latin, that he was accordingly admitted to teach grammar boys wherever he pleased in the diocese and so subscribed the articles. Presentments, call books and exhibit books (recording those who were called and attended, with

details of the licences exhibited) and the various categories of documents concerned with the subsequent enforcement of discipline –
court books, citation books and cause papers: all these are likely to
yield information about schoolmasters, and they have hardly been
touched for this purpose as yet.

For the distribution and variety of schools in particular areas at
particular points in time the written replies to the visitor's articles are
especially important in the eighteenth and early nineteenth centuries.
Very few have been printed. Two well-known exceptions are the
returns for Bishop Secker's visitation of Oxford diocese in 1738 [32]
and those for Archbishop Herring's visitation of York diocese in
1743 [33]. The third of Herring's eleven articles asks: 'Is there any
public or Charity School, endow'd, or otherwise maintain'd in your
Parish? What number of Children are taught in it? And what Care is
taken to instruct them in the Principles of the Christian Religion,
according to the Doctrine of the Church of England; and to bring
them duly to Church, as the Canon requires?' Of the returns from 645
parishes and chapelries in Yorkshire, 266 make no mention of a school.
Where there was a school the return sometimes gives the number of
children, the amount of the endowment (if any), the weekly fees, the
master's other sources of income (often he was the parish clerk as well).
Apart from information about schools the returns give the number of
families in the parish – and so some indication of the population
(against which school provision has to be seen), and also some indication of the educational standards of the parish clergy and the numbers
of them who taught private schools or were masters or ushers in
endowed grammar schools.

The answers to Archbishop Herring's third article are usually brief.
'There is none,' is the terse reply of the parson of Marton (West Riding,
Yorkshire) [34]. 'We have no school, only a poor Woman teaches a few
small children to read, and say the Catechism,', reports the parson of
Moor Monkton, near York [35]. At Hoyland (West Riding, Yorkshire),
with about ninety families, 'We have no publick school but Lady
Malton maintains a School Master to teach English & Writing to such
Boys & Girls as she thinks proper to send.' [36] Some are more
informative. At Hartshead near Dewsbury: 'There is a Charity School
endow'd wth ten Pounds p. Ann., in wch. eighteen poor Children,
haveing Books, Pen's, Ink & paper found 'em, are taught English,
Writing & Arithmetick, till they be of a competent Age to be put out
Apprentices.' [37] The master of Archbishop Holgate's Grammar

School at Hemsworth (West Riding, Yorkshire) replied at unusual length in self-exculpation not only because the school had then no scholars but also because the archbishop was the patron. Besides the school he held a vicarage eight miles away (without a curate) and also a rectory in Northamptonshire. The school had an endowment income of £32 a year and was for the free education of the children of Hemsworth and three neighbouring rural hamlets in Latin, Greek and Hebrew. During his eleven years at the school he had never had more than two scholars at any time from Hemsworth and none at all from the other three places, and this, he says, was because each had a petty school which satisfied local needs. 'There really are none qualified for Grammatical Instruction, within the Compass of our Parish,' he complains. His pupils had been mainly private boarders who had come with him from his previous schools in Nottinghamshire. These had now gone and he had none, but 'to prevent . . . any Suggestions of Disregard' he hired 'a Person, sober & well qualified to teach the Languages & Accompts', paying him half the endowment income [38]. Here in one answer to a visitation article we have light thrown not only on one particular school but also on the many others which shared its dilemma about the same time.

Different in kind from these returns is the account of the diocese of Carlisle which Bishop William Nicolson compiled during his primary visitation in 1703-4. He was as much interested in the schools as in the parish churches and parsonage houses. As often as not he finds the village school in the church, the fittings and monuments defaced by the scholars, and their teacher the parish clerk with no fixed salary for his teaching. The master at Bassenthwaite (Cumberland) is 'hired by ye Neighbouring Hamlets' and teaches in a chapel 'much decay'd in ye Walls and Roof' [39]. At Cumwhitton church (Cumberland) 'The South Window is unglaz'd, and starves the whole Congregation as well as the poor Children; who are here taught . . . by the parish-Clerk.' [40] At Plumland (Cumberland) 'the present Schoolmaster follows ye Plough more than his Books.' [41] Of the grammar schools at Appleby, Penrith and Kirkby Stephen he gives lengthy notes, including a full transcript of the Kirkby Stephen statutes.

In the nineteenth century the Church of England's concern with education sharpened as its traditional role was threatened by the competition of nonconformity and the intervention of the State. Bishops and archdeacons watched even more zealously over educational provision in the parishes under their jurisdiction, and regularly collected information about it. Attention has recently been drawn in the Society's *Bulletin* to the newly discovered returns made by the parishes of the archdeaconry of York in 1815 to a National Society inquiry into local schools, and the reply from one incumbent quoted as an example shows the great value of these returns as source material [42]. Throughout the century visitation articles called for details about Sunday schools, day schools and, in the diocese of York in the 1850s and 1860s, evening classes for early school-leavers and adults. In some dioceses, Lincoln and Ely, for example, boards of education with diocesan inspectors of Church schools produced other records and reports.

All this archive material was produced or preserved at diocesan level. At the level of the parish the Church produced other documents, civil as well as ecclesiastical, which sometimes furnish information about education. The registers of baptisms, marriages and burials, which in about one parish in eight date from 1538 when they were first ordered to be kept, may supply details about local schoolmasters. One buried in Hull in 1572 is described in the register as 'scholem' of ye town and phisicion', which is the only evidence there is that this particular man practised physic. The seventeenth-century Hull registers yield the names of petty schoolmasters, scriveners, writing masters and 'mathematicians', otherwise unknown. Fortunately many parish registers are available in print [43]. The new-style marriage registers introduced after Lord Hardwicke's Marriage Act of 1753, requiring both brides and grooms to sign their names or make their marks, offer – with some qualifications – the best evidence there is for changes in the level of literacy [44]. Basic literacy is one of the first fruits of education and it is remarkable that educational historians have shown so little interest in attempting to assess it.

Besides the registers, the parish chest may contain the accounts and other papers of the churchwardens and the overseers of the poor, which occasionally supply incidental information about local education. More rarely, there may be records of the trustees of an eighteenth-century charity school. At Eastrington in the East Riding the extensive parish records include a copy of the will founding a free school in 1726 and miscellaneous papers relating to its management over a period of 150 years until it was taken over by the new school board in 1878. The nineteenth-century National school may have left behind among the parish records such documents as the site conveyance, the building plan, the trust deed, lists of subscribers, the managers' minute books and cash books, the head teacher's log books [45]. These are not strictly

ecclesiastical records, but the Church has been their custodian because
the parish was the chief unit of civil as well as ecclesiastical administration from Tudor times until the reform of local government in the
late nineteenth century.

Schoolmaster's Licence
Granted to Robert Pell, master of Hull Grammar School by
Archbishop Richard Sterne 16 January 1676

Richardus providentia divina Eboracensis Archiepiscopus Angliae Primas
et Metropolitanus Dilecto Nobis in Christo Roberto Pell literato salutem
gratiam et benedictionem. Ad officium Magistri sive Informatoris
liberae grammaticalis scholae de Kingston super Hull in Comitatu
Eboracensi nostrae Eboracensis Dioecesios et Jurisdictionis ad quod per
gubernatores ejusdem scholae nobis praesentatus existis te (subscriptis
prius et juratis singulis articulis et juramentis per te de jure in hac
praesente subscribendis et jurandis) admittimus ad docendum ignorantes
et erudiendum pueros et adolescentulos in rudimentis grammaticae in
libera schola praedicta necnon authores sive libros quoscunque privilegio
huius regni Angliae autoritateque sufficienter editos et impressos
praelegendum ceteraque omnia et singula quae ad munus et officium
ludimagistri seu puerorum instructoris dictae liberae scholae spectant
et pertinent seu spectare et pertinere dignoscuntur faciendum
exercendum expediendum exequendum et observandum necnon
stipendium sive salarium annuale magistro sive informatori dictae
liberae scholae grammaticalis debitum seu solvitum consuetudine ac
omnia alia jura perspicua commoditates et advantagia eidem
quovismodo spectanda seu spectare debentur recipiendum percipiendum
et habendum. Tibi de cujus litterarum scientia morum probitate
sanaque doctrina plurimum confidimus licentiam et facultatem nostram
concedimus teque ludimagistrum ibidem praeficimus ordinamus et
deputamus per praesentes quamdiu in dicto tuo officio te laudabiliter
gesseris vel donec et quousque aliud a nobis inde habueris in mandatis.
In cujus rei testimonium sigillum nostrum Archiepiscopale praesentibus
apponi fecimus. Datum apud manerium nostrum de Bishopthorpe
decimo sexto die mensis Januarii Anno Domini (Stilo Angliae)
millesimo sexcentesimo septuagesimo sexto nostraeque Translationis
anno decimo tertio.

                                                      Rich. Ebor

Hull Guildhall, Bench Book vii, fos. 496-7.

Note. Words abbreviated by contraction or suspension in the MS have
been extended in the transcript.

Notes

1 The main categories are listed in The Pilgrim Trust's 'Survey of Ecclesiastical Archives' (typescript, 1951), though the details about location are now out of date. J.S. Purvis, *An Introduction to Ecclesiastical Records* (London, 1953), gives examples of the main forms.
2 *Calendar of Inquisitions*, iii (1912), pp.335-6.
3 E.L.C. Mullins, *Texts And Calendars: an Analytical Guide . . .* (London, 1958), gives lists (now out of date).
4 York, Borthwick Institute, Reg. Giffard, fo. 120v, quoted A.F. Leach, *Early Yorkshire Schools*, 2 vols (Yorks. Arch. Soc., 1899, 1903), i, p. 80m.
5 W. Brown and A. Hamilton Thompson, *The Register of William Greenfield . . . 1306-1315*, 4 vols (Surtees Soc., 1931-8), iv, pp. 325, 335-6.
6 A.F. Leach, *Educational Charters* (Cambridge, 1911), pp. 330 ff.
7 A.T. Bannister, *Registrum Thome Spofford 1422-48* (Canterbury and York Soc., 1919), pp. 281-8; *Registrum . . . Johannis Stanbury 1453-74* (Canterbury and York Soc., 1919), pp. 21-33, 105-11.
8 York, Borthwick Institute, Reg. Holgate, fos. 53-57v.
9 A.F. Leach, *Memorials of Beverley Minster: the Chapter Act Book . . .* 2 vols (Surtees Soc., 1898-1903).
10 Ibid. i, pp. 42, 157, 292; ii, pp. 5, 113.
11 Ibid. ii, pp. 127-8.
12 Ibid. i, pp. 42-3, 48, 108, 114-15, 169.
13 Ibid. i, pp. 157-9.
14 A.J. Camp, *Wills and their whereabouts* (Canterbury, 1963), is the best guide.
15 W.K. Jordan, *Philanthropy in England 1480-1660* (London, 1959), pp. 22 ff., discusses wills as historical evidence.
16 *Testamenta Eboracensia*, 6 vols (Surtees Soc., 1836-1902), ii, p. 209.
17 Ibid. ii, p. 270.
18 Ibid. i, p. 157.
19 Ibid. ii, p. 101
20 Ibid. v, p. 279.
21 Ibid. iii, p. 309; iv. p. 25.
22 J.S. Purvis, *The Archives of York Diocesan Registry* (London, 1952), briefly outlines the early York classification. Lincoln is better served by Kathleen Major, *Handlist of the Records of the Bishop of Lincoln and of the Archdeacons of Lincoln and Stow* (Oxford, 1953). For educational examples from the York registry see J.S. Purvis, *Educational Records* (York, 1959).
23 E.H. Carter, *The Norwich Subscription Books . . . 1637-1800* (London, 1937).

24   Hull Guildhall, Bench Book vi, fo. 495.
25   York, Borthwick Institute, R. iv. B. e.11, fo. 22v.
26   York, Borthwick Institute, Subscription Book 1676-83, p.9.
27   Hull Guildhall, Bench Book vi, fos. 496-7.
28   A manuscript directory of schoolmasters compiled from the York records by Dr J.S. Purvis is available for reference in the Borthwick Institute.
29   Early examples in W.H. Frere, *Visitation Articles and Injunctions of the Period of the Reformation,* 3 vols (London, 1910) and W.P.M. Kennedy, *Elizabethan Episcopal Administration,* 3 vols (London, 1924).
30   Susan Capron, 'List of Visitation Records in the York Diocesan Registry' (thesis, Diploma in Archive Administration, Univ. of London, 1956).
31   York, Borthwick Institute, R.VI.A.1, fos. 38-107; extracts in J.S. Purvis, *Tudor Parish Documents of the Diocese of York* (Cambridge, 1948), pp. 104-8.
32   H.A. Lloyd Jukes, *Articles of Enquiry . . . at the Primary Visitation of Dr Thomas Secker 1738* (Oxford Record Soc., 1957).
33   S.L. Ollard and P.C. Walker, *Archbishop Herring's Visitation Returns,* 5 vols (Yorks. Arch. Soc., 1928-31).
34   Ibid. ii, p. 175.
35   Ibid. ii, p. 174.
36   Ibid. ii, p. 55.
37   Ibid. ii, p. 34.
38   Ibid. ii, pp. 45-6.
39   R.S. Ferguson, *Miscellany Accounts of the Diocese of Carlisle . . . by William Nicolson, late Bishop . . .* (Cumb. and Westmorland Antiq. and Arch. Soc., 1877), p. 80.
40   Ibid. p. 112.
41   Ibid. p. 89.
42   *History of Education Society Bulletin,* No.2 (Autumn 1968), pp. 54-5, No. 3 (Spring 1969), pp. 58-60.
43   Some lists in Mullins. The Parish Register Section of the Yorkshire Archaeological Society now numbers 134 volumes.
44   W.P. Baker, *Parish Registers and Illiteracy in East Yorkshire* (East Yorks. Local History Soc., 1961).
45   See generally W.E. Tate, *The Parish Chest,* 3rd ed. (Cambridge, 1960). M.W. Barley, *Parochial Documents of the Archdeaconry of the East Riding* (Yorks. Arch. Soc., 1939), is a classified inventory of parish-chest records, including those about schools, in one area.

MARGARET BRYANT

Topographical resources: private and secondary education in Middlesex from the sixteenth to the twentieth century

Resources

The example discussed here is the writing of the chapter on private and secondary education from the sixteenth to the twentieth centuries for Volume I of the Victoria County History of **Middlesex** [1]. This certainly afforded problems but may illustrate the design and possible contribution of topographical researches to the history of education.

The first and fundamental problem is the status of topographical studies in history. Do they in fact have any status? How are local and topographical studies to be distinguished?

In his discussion of the work of the National Society in Lancashire [2] Dr Sanderson provides an exemplar of local history – first the identification and exploration of the internal life of communities of a recognizable local scale (in this case the diocese of Chester, and especially Lancashire), and second the examination of the tension between the national will as embodied in government policy or central directive (in this case the National Society) and its interpretation, execution and modification by these local communities. This study of the life within local societies and the interplay between them and the larger society or community gives us the characteristic disclosures of this essential branch of history. We discover what did happen rather than what was supposed to be done. We substantiate or actualize, or weaken and destroy, the large statements of legislative, administrative, academic or social intent which so often seem to comprise the history of education.

Topographical history cannot always be identified with either kind of local history and it is long since the boundaries of Middlesex have had more than artificial or perhaps legal and somewhat arbitrary administrative significance. This of course did not alter the time-honoured brief of the Victoria County History, and the editors solved their problems with a good deal of sense and ingenuity. The *Middlesex* volumes handed over to *London* volumes when reorganization transferred specific responsibility from one body to another. But this did not solve the problems of this particular research, it made them worse, for while Professor Ross could bring the story of the education of the working class to a graceful and logical conclusion in 1870 [3], and Professor Bellott was enabled by the blessed concept of academic freedom to bring the history of the University of London down to the present day [4], my assignment was left as an aspect of schooling which sometimes must end in 1902 and sometimes continue further into the twentieth century. Moreover, the research was also hampered by difficulties of definition. The Victoria County History must conform to a well-established frame of reference, which perhaps reflects the preoccupation and undue awe with which historians have approached endowments of any kind. These were to receive individual treatment and the general course of the development of secondary education was to be discussed without reference to the only public and enduring provision for it. At any hint, even whiff, of endowment, this investigation was to consider itself as trespassing. In this way the history of education within a sometimes arbitrarily selected part of the London suburbs was supposed to be achieved by adding up separate parts or aspects; it was a mixture, not a compound, and (if a personal note is permitted) I was often left like Pigling Bland longing to get across the county boundary or like that other equally important little pig gazing wistfully at a notice saying 'Trespassers Will'.

This was only the beginning of the troubles. When it came to sources, the very definition of this brief precluded the existence of the historian's most necessary and characteristic documents – archives. Apart from the vague (and it turned out also almost vain) hope that individual private schools might have left administrative papers, not a trace of what Professor V.H. Galbraith described so aptly and so inelegantly as the secretions of an organism [5] was to be seen. Yet right from the beginning it was clear that there *was* an organism; puffings and snufflings could be heard if not seen; deep breathings in the suburban undergrowth were all around.

I

The only possible plan of attack was therefore to plunge into the jungle and hack a way through. The approach had to be parish by parish, beginning with wider surveys such as the Rev. Daniel Lysons, *The Environs of London, Being an Historical Account of the Towns, Villages and Hamlets within Twelve Miles of that Capital* (1792-6) and *An Historical Account of those Parishes in the County of Middlesex, which are not Described in the Environs of London* (1800). Lysons usually only records the presence of private schools incidentally. In his extracts from parish registers he may mention that a house once inhabited by an eminent family has become a school. In Newington the house of General Fleetwood, Cromwell's son-in-law, had in 1795 become a ladies' boarding school in the occupation of Mrs Crisp. Sections on manorial descent also show how large old houses – Lincoln House at Enfield, for example – were used as schools. Only a few well-established private schools are given direct mention – Hackney School, for example, is described as 'having flourished nearly a century on the same spot'; its fame for dramatic performances is mentioned, but this arises from the connection of the school-keepers with the holders of the vicarage. Hackney dissenting college is also named in connection with the Presbyterian congregation [6] . In Edward Wedlake Brayley's, *London and Middlesex, or an Historical, Commercial and Descriptive Survey of the Metropolis of Great Britain, including Sketches of its Environs etc.* (1810) and its fourth and fifth volumes by the Rev. Joseph Nightingale and J. Norris Brewer (1815, 1816), schools are sometimes mentioned as a feature of a parish or district. Highgate's many respectable boarding schools included 'an establishment for the education of the sons of Jews', patronized by families of the 'first consequence' and including a synagogue in its 'spacious buildings' [7] .

James Thorne, *Handbook to the Environs of London*, alphabetically arranged, 2 vols. (1876), tends to describe schools as part of the apparatus of a parish or district. Christ's College at Finchley, for example, is said to have been founded by the present rector with a view to providing a first-class education at a moderate cost' [8] .

Next histories of individual parishes or of areas of suburban development had to be searched, for example Thomas Faulkner, *History and Antiquities of Brentford, Ealing and Chiswick* (1845) and *Kensington* (1820); William Robinson, *History and Antiquities of the Parish of Stoke Newington* (1820) and of *Hackney* (1842) and *Tottenham*, 2nd ed. (1840); George Redford and Thomas Hurry Riches, *The History of the Ancient Town of Uxbridge* (1818; reprinted 1895); Charles Lethbridge Kingsford, *The Early History of Piccadilly, Leicester Square and Soho*, Publication No.55 of the London Topographical

Society (Cambridge, 1925); and Millicent Rose, *The East End of London* (London, 1951). These varied widely in reliability and value but in this research at least the earlier more antiquarian works were often useful in expanding, correcting (even contradicting) sometimes corroborating, the equally antiquarian Lysons or Wedlake Brayley, and as they were nearly all later in date there was less likelihood of mere repetition and copying, for the enthusiastic local specialist would rarely rely altogether or quite uncritically on the more general survey. Some rather later examples were outstandingly useful, especially S. Lewis, Junior, *The History and Topography of the Parish of St Mary, Islington* (1842) and William J. Pinks, *History of Clerkenwell*, with additions by Edward Wood (ed.) (1865). But the earlier antiquarian tradition continued in works such as J.B. Ellenor, *Rambling Recollections of Chelsea and the Surrounding District* (1901). At this stage, however, all had to be grist (or at least temporary grist) to the topographical mill.

The third class of topographical materials was directories, either of the general kind, such as Peter Barfoot and John Wilkes, *The Universal British Directory of Trade, Commerce and Manufacture* (1791-7) (schoolkeeping was classed with these), *Kelly's* and the *Post Office Directories*; or specialist scholastic directories, for example G.B. Whittaker, *The Boarding School and London Masters' Directory or the Addresses of the First Teachers in Every Department of Education, and of the Principal Finishing and Preparatory Seminaries of Young Ladies and Gentleman in and near the Metropolis* (1828); Crockford's *Scholastic Directory* for 1861, 'Being an Annual Work to Reference for Facts relating to Educators, Education and Educational Establishments (Public and Private) in the UK'; and an invaluable military gentleman, Captain F.S. de Carteret-Bisson, F.R.G.S., M.S.A., author of *Our Schools and Colleges*, [Vol.1] (London, 1872); [Vol.1], 4th ed. (London, 1879), Part VI, 'Concerning our Endowed and all the leading Schools of Great Britain'; Vol.II: *For Girls* (London, 1884), Part VIII, 'Concerning our Endowed Schools and our Higher and Middle Class Private Schools and Colleges'. There is also the much more sketchy *Hampton's Scholastic Directory and Hotel Guide* (1893-4). Recent or current directories of the same type were useful for corroboration, etc. From the mid-nineteenth century also there began the *Catholic Directories*, e.g. *The Laity's Directory* (1835-6). Directories often contained another type of evidence which had to be used considerably – advertisements – and there was also a useful miscellany including these – the two volumes of Lysons's *Collectanea* in the British Museum. For newspaper advertisements the use of an unpublished thesis saved much time: Esther Greenberg, *Contribution to Education of Private Schools in the First Half of the Nineteenth Century* (University of London, King's College, M.A. 1953). This employed the technique of sampling the advertisements in *The Times* at carefully spaced dates.

'Local collections', usually at the borough libraries, were useful, if entirely fortuitous and haphazard, containing sometimes advertisements, press cuttings, prospectuses, speech-day addresses and even a very few administrative papers – bills and so forth of little real use. Catalogues of local exhibitions arranged by the National Register of Archives were also very useful and contained material which had since disappeared.

As the scene became more crowded and confused in the nineteenth century there was help from official surveys which had been organized topographically. Here there was danger of trespassing on endowments, or on the provision of schools from above by a class of persons not intending to use them for their own offspring, but as strict adherence to instructions would have meant that significant areas of education were ignored in the overall plan, a certain amount of cautious smuggling had to take place. Surveys of this kind included *The Education Enquiry Abstracts* of 1818, 1833 and 1835 [9]; the *Reports from the Select Committees on Education* of 1834 and 1835 which recorded much provision of education by private venture [10]. However this was education of the poor and for the County History was Professor Ross's concern. Then there was the *Census of 1851* with Horace Mann's magnificent labours (the volume on *Education, England and Wales*, was published in 1854) [11]; the *Report of the Commission on Popular Education in England* (The Newcastle Commission) of 1861, Part III containing the report by Josiah Wilkinson on three representative poor-law unions in the Metropolitan district, St Pancras, St George-in-the-East and Chelsea [12]; and the *Report of the Schools' Inquiry (Taunton) Commission* of 1868. The report of the Taunton Commission was particularly valuable, for Middlesex was chosen as one of the counties surveyed by an Assistant Commissioner, the H.M.I., D.R. Fearon, who made an acute assessment of the educational needs of the various sections of the suburbs and the different levels of 'middle-class education' provided or deficient [13]. It is surprising that more use has not been made of these reports by local historians – whether educational specialists or not. Finally, *The Return of Pupils in Public,*

Private, Secondary and Other Schools (not being Public Elementary or Technical Schools) in England and the Teaching Staff of such Schools on 1 June 1897 [14] provided the only reasonably complete and reliable survey made at the end of Victoria's reign, when the jungle had become thickest and most entangled. With these official topographically arranged surveys it is perhaps reasonable to include Charles Booth's *Life and Labour of the People in London* (1890) in which Llewellyn Smith made a survey of urban and suburban education [15].

Other official inquiries, while not making any special study of the Middlesex area, provided valuable local material in their minutes of evidence. These included *The Bryce Commission on Secondary Education* of 1895 [16] and *The Special Report from the Select Committee on the Teachers' Registration and Organization Bill* (4 July 1891) [17]. *The Report of a Conference on Secondary Education convened by the Vice Chancellor of the University of Cambridge* in 1896 offered parallel or complementary discussion from an unofficial source.

The setting-up of the Board of Education in 1899 at last opened some chance of archival evidence. The so-called *List 60, of Secondary Schools in England Recognized as Efficient* (1907-8) [18] led to a limited number of *Board of Education School Files*, while the Board's *Special Reports on Educational Subjects* sometimes contained invaluable illustrative material — for example Sadler on preparatory schools made a case study of a school in Hampstead, Heddon Court, Rosslyn Hill [19].

Before leaving these rather broadly defined topographical documents the apparent neglect of the most characteristic evidence of this type — maps — must be mentioned. But the exact location of individual schools was rarely of significance and the general background of suburban expansion in relation to the overall distribution of schools could largely be presupposed in this context. Only perhaps a real gluttony for work would have necessitated the checking of the claims of various advertisements for schools on 'deep beds of gravel' against the geological surveys.

Local newspapers were another valuable source, but a systematic search was impossible for reasons of time, and here also trails had to be followed up from other types of document. *The Gentleman's Magazine* and *Notes and Queries* were as usual a mine of rather haphazard information. *The Transactions of the London & Middlesex Archaeological Society*, however, yielded little useful material.

II

Those various types of topographical document led on to others. First *The Dictionary of National Biography* was an obvious source, though it was a matter of chance whether private education was considered important enough for mention (or indeed whether it was correctly described). Dr Nicholas Hans in his *New Trends in Education in the Eighteenth Century* (London, 1951), on the basis of calculating the proportion of entries in the *D.N.B.* educated privately during the latter part of the eighteenth century, put forward the thesis that public schools were less used then for elder than for younger sons and that the private academies of this period represented a recognizable educational renaissance. These Middlesex researches would perhaps modify his thesis somewhat. It appeared that the private schools could suffer not only from being ignored or written off but also from inflated or anachronistic claims being made for them. Overlapping with the *D.N.B.* there were useful trails to be followed in for example *The Proceedings of the Huguenot Society in London*, the specialist denominational societies, and the transactions of, for example, the Chetham Society.

Second, the huge miscellany of literary, autobiographical and other materials could of course have been explored indefinitely, if not systematically, but this was (fortunately) not possible; therefore references were usually followed up from topographical sources or from personal knowledge and even chance encounter. Even so a significant picture did emerge of the literary and intellectual life of the metropolis and its significance for education of all kinds, but especially perhaps for the private sector. This was servicing society and the economy at all levels as well as sometimes enriching the personal life, but its particular danger was its very private and expedient nature, and the possibility of intellectual, civilized discourse to some extent drew it into the public arena. The community of letters was a very real force in the eighteenth and early nineteenth centuries. Literary booksellers played an important part and Middlesex schoolmasters had the advantage of easy access to the world of books and printing as well as that of men of letters. A perhaps obvious but irresistible example is the friendship of Dr Johnson for such private school-keepers as Dr Charles Burney, a notable Greek scholar, son of his old friend the musician, who had a school at Hammersmith which alas escaped across the river to Greenwich; and for the Episcopalian Scot, James Elphinston, who had an important academy in Kensington: 'I would not put a boy to him whom I intended for a man of learning, but for the sons of citizens who are to learn a little, get good morals and then go to trade he may do very well.' Dr William Rose, translator of Sallust, who had a prosperous school in Chiswick from 1758 till his death in 1786, Johnson praised for his scholarship, but blamed for his leniency: 'What the boys gain at one end they lose at the other.' Johnson took an interest also in the career of Dr Samuel Parr (1747-1825) who, between being on the staff at Harrow and accepting the headmastership of the endowed school at Colchester, attempted to set up a private academy at Stanmore — literally as a rival to Harrow. Johnson considered this the crisis of Parr's life [20].

A more specific, and significant, example of the kind of encouragement which the intellectual life of the capital gave to essential educational developments was the active help which King's College, especially at first F.D. Maurice, gave to the emergence of Queen's College, Harley Street, from the Governesses' Benevolent Institution in 1848, and which the staff of University College gave to Bedford College for Ladies in 1849 [21]. This research underlined the fact that the whole renaissance of women's education in the nineteenth century was made possible not only by the concentration and mutual support of women reformers in the London suburbs but by the help they could get from wealthy or able and influential men in the City, at the Inns of Court, in academic and official circles, etc., and also among the clergy.

Thirdly, a more educationally significant but not always topographically respectable body of literary evidence, for the provenance of ideas is not usually the significant thing about them, was provided by the numerous treatises on education written by Middlesex school-keepers or teachers at all levels, and popular school books written by them. This material remains largely to be explored but its very quantity and quality confronts and criticizes the extraordinary received wisdom about 'the great educators' in many history of education courses. Examples included Hezekiah Woodward (1590-1675), who kept a school in the City and then at Uxbridge during the Interregnum, and wrote *A Light to Grammar and all the Other Arts and Sciences or the Rule of Practice*, 'proceeding by the clue of nature and conduct of right reason so opening the door thereunto' (1641); and *A Gate of Sciences* 'opened by a natural key or a practical lecture upon the great book of nature whereby the child is able to read the creatures there'. He was a disciple of Comenius and had already described the miserable experiences of his own education (*not* in Middlesex) in his *Child's Patrimony* (1640) and *Child's Portion* (1649) [22]. Robert Ainsworth (1660-1743) ran through a gamut of religious affiliations, from non-juring to Calvinism, and was at the end of his life seen at Methodist prayer meetings, 'like old Simeon, waiting to see the Lord's salvation'. He kept schools in several Middlesex parishes and in 1698 wrote *The Most Natural and Easy Way of Institution* 'containing Proposals for making a Domestic Education less Chargeable to Parents and More Easy and Beneficial to Children' [23].

The nonconformist academies produced a whole range of important works of this kind. An early example was Joshua Oldfield's *Essay Towards the Improvement of Reason* (1707). He taught at one of the early Hoxton Square academies (fl. 1699 to about 1729) and outlined a complete scheme of education – logic, modern geography, history, chronology, laws (including international and commercial law), current affairs, some astronomy and navigation, mathematics, a thorough study of English and the principles of religion. Vocational studies for lawyers, ministers and doctors would include civil law, Hebrew and New Testament Greek, ethics, mathematics and natural philosophy, with 'experiments'. He also discussed methods of teaching and was noted for his liberal and tolerant approach. Oldfield's mathematical learning 'met with the approbation of the great Sir Isaac Newton' and he met and may even have influenced John Locke [24].

At the other end of the century the *Works* of Middlesex's perhaps most daring innovator in both the theory and practice of education, Joseph Priestley, need detailed examination, perhaps especially in our case for their ideas and practical suggestions for the teaching of history [25]. Works by private school-keepers include Dr William Barrow's *An Essay on Education in which are Particularly Considered the Merits and Defects of the Discipline in our Academies* (1802), based on his Oxford prize essay on *Academical Education*. He taught at and was master of the famous Soho Square Academy, esteemed as 'the senior academy', which may have had a continuous history from the last decade of the seventeenth century until the 1820s. Its pupils included artists such as Rowlandson and Turner, Edmund Burke's beloved son, and one of James Boswell's sons before he went to Westminster [26].

William Johnstone, master of an academy at Stanmore, in 1818 published the *Result of Experience in the Practice of Instruction, or Hints for the Improvement of the Art of Tuition as regards the Middling and Higher Classes of Society.* He claimed that at least 1,500 boys had passed through his hands, to have tested his own and other people's theories by experiment, and had also visited other schools and so to have 'taken pains to ascertain both by trial and enquiry the chief merits of the few variations which he has perceived between the plans of . . . numerous teachers'. The curriculum and methods which he advocated as a result of this early plan of educational research are remarkably enlightened. His description of an 'Encyclopaediac Course of Liberal Education' and his attention to the capacity of the pupil and the importance of illustration and explanation are reminders that these were still the days of the Enlightenment and of Rousseau's influence [27].

Another such writer was the forebear of an important educational family. Moses Miall kept an academy in the old Sandys house at Islington, and in 1822 published *Practical Remarks on Education* advocating kindly relationships between teacher and taught and showing psychological insight well in advance of his age. His school does not seem to have been a financial success [28]. The nonconformist Rev. John Evans, also an Islington schoolmaster for thirty years, wrote in 1798 an *Essay on the Education of Youth* which emphasized the importance of science in the curriculum and advertisements for his school claimed that lectures on for example optics and electricity were given 'illustrated with valuable and complete apparatus' [29].

III

To discover, structure, interpret and criticize all these sources, this research like most other research, perhaps even more so, was indebted to the references in a wide range of specialist secondary works, including R.L. Archer, *Secondary Education in the Nineteenth Century* (1921); Foster Watson, *The Beginnings of the Teaching of the Modern Subjects in England* (1909); J.W. Adamson, *Pioneers of Modern Education* (1902); K. Lambley, *The Teaching and Cultivation of the French Language in England during Tudor and Stuart Times* (1920); J.W. Ashley Smith, *The Birth of Modern Education* (1954) and G.A. Beck (ed.), *The English Catholics 1850-1950* (1950). It is perhaps safe to say that older works tended to emphasize the unity of educational provision, to discuss the private or independent sectors alongside such public provision as existed. Except for example for specialist denominational studies, more recent works [30] often concentrate on institutional aspects, sometimes even seem to be mesmerized by those institutions which appear to be successful or dominant today. For this reason reprints of older works would appear to be especially valuable.

IV

Before turning to the much more important and interesting discussion of the value of these various categories of evidence and of what significance emerged from them, two disappointments must be mentioned. First the Licences of Schoolmasters in the Diocese of London Vicars' General Books [31] bore little or no relation to what was happening in the county, according at any rate to the disclosures of other types of document. The identifiable overlap between those known to be teaching and those licensed to do so was minimal. It would be most interesting to hear other people's experience in this respect. Admittedly the anonymity afforded by city and suburb was already a powerful factor, but they were also as near as could be to the seat of authority and power [32]. A second disappointment was that, when institutions to service private education began to emerge, even these failed in the matter of archives. The College of Preceptors, that curious Victorian improvisation, which took up its headquarters in this county in 1848, had either destroyed or lost its archives. Systematic use of its journal, *The Educational Times* (from 2 October 1847), would no doubt yield valuable information, and the management and policy of the college certainly showed that characteristic social and vocational urgency in schooling which the suburbs so vividly illustrate [33].

Findings

What did emerge from this jungle, or rather, perhaps, what was found in it? I never found Professor Galbraith's archive secreting organism, but the puffings in the undergrowth were real enough. Studying suburban education in this manner by the use of varied documents which tended to make up in *quantity* what they lacked in *quality*, disclosed the strength and extraordinary variety and vitality of the appetite for education (or perhaps schooling) both economic, social, even intellectual, in that 'mobile, expanding, usually prosperous and always aspiring society' [34], while stronger even than fad or fashion was the operation of the largest and most diversified labour market in the world. It perhaps required little research to realize that the suburbs formed a kind of forcing house for educational development, but the results did give a more precise and detailed view of the scene, capable of much more exact and productive analysis. The social *demand* for education at what we should today call the secondary level and the personal need for it, whether the need is intellectual or vocational, even moral and emotional, could be critically examined and even classified.

I

First, the gap between Government intent and local operation proved wider than even I had suspected, strongly emphasizing the need for local research to substantiate large and precarious generalizations. For example, the continuing tradition of conventual education for girls remained strong even in non-Catholic families, and during the penal era Roman Catholic families were assisted by the operation, in the inner suburbs, of Mary Ward and her companions, the principal organizers of such schools in England and on the Continent. The protection of the court was important but was certainly not the only reason for their survival, and after 1669 such a school at Hammersmith not only claimed continuity in the London area throughout the Interregnum, but during the Popish Plot era and later in the Gordon Riots was protected from molestation by the local tradespeople. It was an accepted and fashionable local institution and had some non-Catholic pupils [35].

The same was true of the nonconformist academies. During the active period of the Clarendon Code they were already numerous in Middlesex, even in the inner suburbs — some had to move frequently and some were nominally kept by the wives of ejected clergy — but after a surprisingly brief period of this kind many settled down to become established local institutions, especially in Islington and the neighbouring parishes — a Presbyterian congregation was established here from 1660 and ministers could combine 'pulpit labours' with tutoring [36].

II

The significance and influence of these nonconformist academies was strongly reinforced by this topographical approach — and probably the interaction of the many examples so close together and the concentration of demand for this kind of education heightened their significance as an aspect of the European Enlightenment. Their encouragement of learning by explanation and free inquiry, the evolution within them of a new and wider conception of the curriculum of both higher secondary and further vocational education, and their contribution to the understanding of education as a continuous and active process, were all confirmed. In Middlesex this connection with the Age of Reason is agreeably underlined by the dramatic demise of Hackney College, the last of these academies attempting to offer a wide and open secondary education both for future ministerial candidates and other pupils. Its failure was due not only to its over 'superb a style', 'inconsistent with the plainness and simplicity of the Dissenters', but also to the loss of confidence, amounting almost to panic, engendered by the appointment of tutors considered to be not only unorthodox but of Jacobin sympathies – Richard Price, Gilbert Wakefield, Joseph Priestley. Finally it became impossible to control the students, drunk with the bliss of being alive in that particular dawn. They gave a Republican supper with Tom Paine as guest, they called for 'Ça ira' in a London theatre instead of 'God Save the King'. 'Babylon is fallen' cried a profoundly relieved and orthodox dissenter when the college was closed.

Fig.1 Highbury College, Islington (an engraving from 1842). This theological college grew out of lectures given by the Societas Evangelica. (From S. Lewis, *History of Islington*.)

The institutional legacy which these academies bequeathed to the London suburbs was the theological college, e.g. New College in Hampstead, whose interactions with London University are particularly interesting to historians, and Highbury College. The importance for the established Church and for other denominations of the development of a proper and professional ministerial training is nationally rather than locally significant [37].

III

Much light was thrown on what some would call the obstinate vitality of the private school, so marked a characteristic of English education. At the close of the Middle Ages London and its environs were served by 'limited and undistinguished' grammar school resources and the Church resisted petitions for increased provision, but during the sixteenth and seventeenth centuries, to use Professor Jordan's phrase, the 'persistent and continuous generosity' of the City community increased the number of foundations and places for able or aspiring boys until it seems probable that the provision was fully equal to the demand [38]. But this generosity, under the increased prestige of Greek and Roman studies, provided an education that did not satisfy the needs of an expanding economy, a changing society, developments in the machinery of government or new intellectual thrusts. Moreover it had imprisoned the apparatus of education in perpetual corporations which were unable or unwilling to adapt to new needs. The very merchant community which had endowed these freeholds was during the same period in urgent need of supplementary education, especially in modern languages (including the native language), mathematics and navigation, and French schools, often set up by Huguenot refugees, visiting mathematics tutors, etc., were developing in the City and London suburbs during the reign of Elizabeth [39].

From this point the story of boys' private schools developed always in relation to that of the endowed and 'public' schools. It is possible to discern recognizable but of course overlapping periods in their history.

1. It is not in the early period easy to draw the line between schools and visiting masters or tutors who 'taught abroad' and the vocational element, and the attendance of pupils of widely varying ages for short-term objectives — a good hand, merchant accompts by the Italian method, shorthand, the French language, etc. — is very strong. The

Fig. 2 Seventeenth-century writing-master's trade card, from More's *Writing Master's Assistant* (1696?). (From Ambrose Heal, *The English Writing-Masters and their Copy Books 1570-1800* (Cambridge University Press, 1931).)

most highly specialized example I came across was William Leekey (1710?-1746) who moved his school from Cripplegate to Wapping and then back to the City, and advocated a different method of writing for 'men of bulky size and ladies laced in their stays' [40]. These 'Penmen' and mathematics masters are not always easy to distinguish and some also added improved and more rapid systems for teaching Latin — again, probably for 'crash courses'. Connections with seafaring and military studies were strong. Pepys's interest in mathematics tutors is well known and his lists are an important source about them. At the outset of the eighteenth century the school in Bethnal Green kept by Samuel Morland, dissenter and classical scholar, had as mathematics tutor William Jones (1675-1749), father of the orientalist, who had worked in a counting house and taught mathematics aboard a man-of-war. He was a friend of Newton and author of a *New Compendium of the Whole Art of Navigation*. A later example, John Bonnycastle (1750?-1821), author of several works on elementary mathematics, had an academy in Hackney and later became professor of mathematics at the Royal Military Academy at Woolwich [41]. Some academies specialized in military or navigational studies — for example John Bettesworth's Naval Academy, opened in 1782 in Ormond House,

Chelsea [42], and Lochée's Military Academy in the same area from about 1770 [43].

During this first period, therefore, such 'academies' provided wide and varied courses but the approach was *à la carte* rather than *table d'hôte*. A representative specimen is that of William Watts which began as a City 'writing school' and moved to Soho in about 1739. It claimed that young men

... intended for military employment are instructed in fortification, gunnery, surveying etc., and every other part of knowledge for that profession, as modern languages, riding, fencing, drawing etc. Those who incline to the marine are taught every branch of navigation etc. Those who would be formed for the counting house, learn to write strong and free – to compute with ease, expedition and demonstration – to enter mercantile transactions by double entry – to know the use of all the books kept by merchants with their different methods – to draw all forms of business – the nature of foreign exchange and the proper style of correspondence. The intention of this undertaking being to perfect the instructed in any branch of knowledge in as little a time as capacity and application will admit, therefore they may apply as many hours every day as best fits their conveniency, may board in the Academy or may only dine there [44].

2. Even during this period quite a large proportion of these highly vocational academies also provided something like general secondary education or were used for that purpose, and a number of private schools of a general character grew up side by side with them from the seventeenth century onwards. Sir Ralph Verney placed his second son Jack in Mr Turberville's school in Kensington in 1656, and he was later apprenticed to a Levant merchant for £400. Sir John Reresby went to a 'then famous school for gentlemen's sons', the 'Blew' House at Enfield Chace. Samuel Pepys escorted 'my Lord's' son, Edward, to William Fuller's School at Twickenham in January 1660 [45].

Some of these private schools became established local institutions, a source of income and a sphere of professional skill and concern for a family over several generations. An important and early example was 'Hackney School' or 'Newcome's Academy' which was founded in 1685 by Benjamin Morland, a dissenter who had conformed at the Restoration, and until 1820 it remained in the hands of the descendants and connections of his former pupil Henry Newcome, who went to Cambridge straight from the school, returned as its usher, and in 1714 married Morland's daughter Lydia [46]. Schools of this kind, especially during the eighteenth century, were used for a variety of purposes – as ancillaries, alternatives or preparatory for the endowed schools, even by families who could be expected to patronize the so-called public schools, especially for their younger sons. The wider curriculum and often more kindly and homely treatment may have attracted parents, especially during the brief period much discussed by Professor Musgrove when domestic rather than public education was stressed [47]. An amusing sidelight here is that some schools became almost recognized as appropriate for the illegitimate offspring of Whig or Tory families. Presumably *both* a genuinely domestic *or* a public education would have been embarrassing to all parties [48].

3. As Professor Perkin's 'viable class society' came into being over the turn of the century [49], there is a recognizable, but not sharply delineated, period when the private schools served an emerging middle-class which for this comparatively short time did not wish to be identified with, or merge into, the upper classes. Dr Kitson Clark has indeed emphasized for us the real hatred of the landed aristocracy and the old 'prescriptive society' during this period [50]. This ended when political, social and educational institutions were sufficiently infected or infused with the newer middle-class ethos, though it continued for those ranges of the middle classes who had not the economic resources for higher aspirations, or who were ideologically protected against them.

During this period private schools were essential to the middle-classes and they proliferated and bloomed in the suburbs. The very number of justificatory or explanatory treatises by school-keepers already mentioned relates to this newly self-conscious demand. A reminder of the dangers of using this kind of evidence was a rather delightful parody of such prospectuses or advertisements dressed up as educational theory, transcribed recently in the U.S. *History of Education Quarterly* – the *Academy Keeper* of 1770. It purported to tell the story of a hitherto unsuccessful careerist who married a boarding-school keeper and by 'peculiar attention to the tempers of the boys and the dispositions of their parents, by a flexibility of face, for which I was always remarkable, the assistance of a northern degree, and a tolerable degree of assiduity' soon 'accumulated a large fortune with credit' [51].

Yet this kind of evidence, together with advertisements, has one infallible revelation to make – what the school-keepers thought the parents wanted. An almost exact parallel in some respects with that spurious example was James Anderson, a Scottish graduate who had an academy at the Mansion House, Hammersmith, from about the 1770s until the end of the century. The school, which then continued until at least 1839, illustrates the first requirement of parents — a broad curriculum but one also vocationally relevant. Anderson included navigation, and his successor Dr B. Duncan, formerly of Highgate Commercial Academy, prepared boys for 'foreign or domestic trade and the public offices' [52].

By this period school fees were usually expected to cover a broad general education which had replaced the older plan of following short intensive courses at special schools, or paying extra for visiting masters. The later part of the school course might then branch out and specialize. At Cherwell House Academy in the Upper Mall at Hammersmith in 1821 Mr Faulkner prepared young gentlemen for 'the Universities, public offices and foreign and domestic commercial business . . . The course of instruction is of a general character in its earlier stages, but is subsequently varied with a view to the particular destination of the pupil.' 'The Grammar Course' was given a subordinate place where 'youth are designed for the counting house', and attention concentrated on the acquiring of 'a good English style, the French language and the principles of trade and commerce, writing with expedition and elegance and a correct knowledge of arithmetic and book-keeping' [53].

Secondly, parents usually wanted their children to be happy and healthy — suburban schools were not after all protected by remoteness and even the florid claims of some prospectuses may have at least corresponded to some extent to intentions. There is evidence that a significant number of middle-class parents preferred competition to replace corporal punishment during this period — apart from anything else advertisements suggested that they preferred disciplinary methods which speeded rather than delayed learning: 'the system pursued, which is peculiarly calculated to excite a spirit of emulation among the pupils, insures the most rapid progress in every branch of education', said the proprietor of College House Academy on Highgate Hill in 1826 [54]. In the open market education could not afford to be useless, slow and painful. Some advertisements almost seem to be trying to sell the whole school. In 1831 Mr Softley of the Manor House Academy in Stoke Newington claimed to have spent £2,000 on improving 'this delightful situation', the children were treated with 'great indulgence'. Six acres of garden, pleasure grounds, noble gravel walks, fives ground, a giant

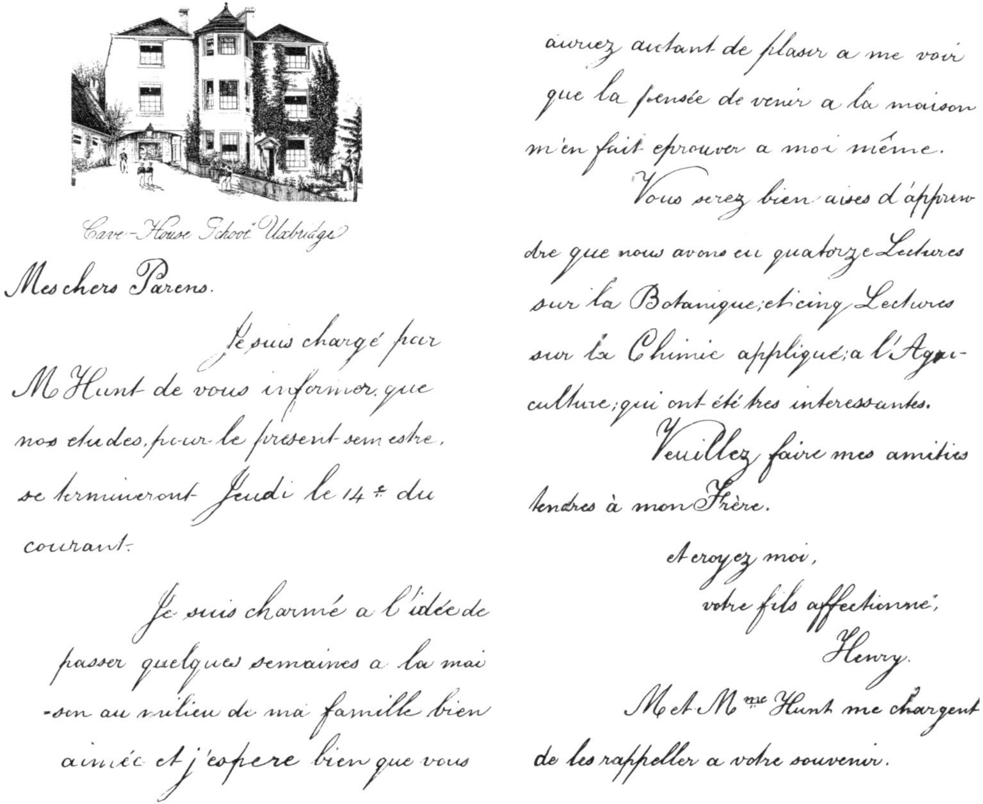

Cave House, Ickenham, Uxbridge

Mes chers Parens.

Je suis chargé par Mr Hunt de vous informer que nos études pour le présent semestre se termineront jeudi le 14e du courant.

Je suis charmé à l'idée de passer quelques semaines à la maison au milieu de ma famille bien aimée et j'espère bien que vous aurez autant de plaisir à me voir que la pensée de venir à la maison m'en fait éprouver à moi même.

Vous serez bien aise d'apprendre que nous avons eu quatorze Lectures sur la Botanique et cinq Lectures sur la Chimie appliquée à l'Agriculture, qui ont été très intéressants.

Veuillez faire mes amitiés tendres à mon Frère.

Croyez moi,
votre fils affectionné,
H. Henry.

Mr et Mme Hunt me chargent de les rappeler à votre souvenir.

Fig. 3 A boy at Uxbridge Grammar School, Cave House (a private school), writes in 1854 to his parents in French (one suspects from a copy) and describes courses of lectures in science. (From Uxbridge Library Local Collection, no. 765B.)

stride, an observatory and a cricket field were dwelt upon, as well as the domestic arrangements on a liberal scale, and the course of tuition which included 'everything necessary for an entrance into the public schools, colleges, counting house, etc.' [55]. The young gentlemen induced to return here at the beginning of each term may not have endorsed the claims of the advertisement, but schooling of this kind clearly had to create and satisfy its own market. The only trouble was that the customer was not the consumer.

Patrick Scott's delightful article in the Society's *Bulletin* [56] on Anstey's *Vice-Versa* as an authentic portrait of a private school of a slightly later period – the 1860s – puts its finger unerringly on the third demand of middle-class parents from such private schools and the one which distinguished them most sharply from the public schools – the need for moral and social supervision. The middle-class parent was simply not prepared to tolerate the public schools' methods in this respect. Leaving large numbers of boys of mixed ages to their own devices led to practices which outraged the middle-class conscience. Until abuses of this kind were reformed, or at least decently formalized, in the prefect system, many parents preferred private schools. This brought its own horrors. In 1842 Mr Robson of the Hyde Side Academy, Edmonton, exhorted his pupils to relieve their studies by amusement, as

> . . . the bow required to be occasionally unstrung . . . We have many places in which you can enjoy the best and most manly of games, cricket; there is a fine piece of water near the premises in which you can under my care learn to swim . . . and on half holidays there is not a nook in this beautiful country that we will not explore. I say we, for I will accompany you to point out the charms of nature, examine with you the subjects of natural history that we may meet with, and blend instruction with exercise. [57]

4. In the mid-nineteenth century what might almost be called a period of systematization of private education can be discerned. This is revealed for example by that rather unpromising category of evidence – the scholastic directory. These for the most part proved to be inaccurate, incomplete, repetitious, and they were certainly more valuable for the sheer volume of evidence which they supplied than for its exactness. But their overall approach and arrangement were significant. *The Boarding School and London Masters' Directory* of 1828 is a reflection of the older private school and visiting master tradition. It describes families crowding into the metropolis, not only

for the season, parliamentary sessions, and so on, but 'on account of the grand work of education', bringing their daughters and sons for the benefit of the 'best London masters' or to be entered for 'some eligible school, where eminent professors may be had upon easier terms than in a private lesson'. It paints a harrowing picture of the extreme exhaustion to which these eminent men were reduced and declares that only the noble consideration of the King in ending the season in July enabled them to recruit their strength at the sea before their engagements with the schools brought them back in the autumn [58]. (Was this, by the way, George IV's sole contribution to the cause of education?)

In 1861 Crockford's *Scholastic Directory* [59] still listed 'Private Schools for Gentlemen' and 'for Ladies' alphabetically under the name of the proprietor, but Bisson's *Directories* of 1872, 1879 and 1884 listed them as institutions, classified according to management and ownership, giving qualifications of staff, the curriculum followed and above all the examinations taken. Even allowing for the Captain's military orderliness and desire to classify, a new conception of these schools is discernible, many of them still private property, but with emerging public responsibility and significance, and with connections with other branches of education [60].

The growth of the professions, the reform of the army and civil service entry and above all the growth of 'middle-class examinations', was the mid-century turning-point in this respect, adding their systematizations and standardizations of learning to the already considerable number of semi-professional examinations for which private schools prepared. The College of Preceptors' examinations of schools began in 1854, the Society of Arts in 1856, the Oxford and Cambridge Locals in 1858. As examples chosen almost at random to illustrate the range of such examinations, in 1858 the Maida Hill College and School was set up to provide direct preparations for the Professions, Commerce, Army, Civil Service and East Indian Examinations, for £100 a year. A year later the Kilburn and St John's Wood Civil and Military Institute prepared for the Indian Civil Service, Indian Engineers, Woolwich, the Staff College, Ceylon Civil Service, Indian Civil Telegraph, Sandhurst, Direct Commissions, Home Civil Service and universities, for £150 a year [61].

Here we are in the presence of either the aspiring middle classes, those who passed even beyond Fearon's schools of 'the first grade', or of ex-public-school products who required cramming before they could enter professions formerly open to purchase and influence. Here the Barbarians are mingling with the Philistines. But more humble schools catered for less aspiring candidates. In 1872 Eagle Hall Collegiate School at Southgate, Edmonton, gave a 'sound English education, preparatory either to Business or Professional life' and put pupils in for 'Civil Service, the Preliminary Medical, the Incorporated Law Society, the Oxford and Cambridge Middle Class and other Examinations' [62]. The College, Tollington Park, added the examinations of the Royal College of Surgeons, Apothecaries' Hall and the Pharmaceutical Society [63]. Both Fearon's assistant commissioner's report and the minutes of evidence of the Schools' Inquiry Commission gave an interesting discussion of the effects of these examinations on the schools [64]. This is a subject on which a great deal of work needs to be done.

5. With the Endowed Schools Act of 1869, and with the subsequent competition from the reformed and expanded public schools, the heyday of the suburban private school was over. Many of course survived, especially for the lower and middle middle classes. Many still came and went. A considerable proportion of the more successful ones adapted themselves as preparatory schools, the development of which as a distinct species is clearly illustrated in the suburbs [65].

The factors which enabled a few schools to survive and adapt themselves to the new competition are well brought out in the contrasted history of two Middlesex schools both founded under the influence of the Philosophic Radicals in the early part of the century. University College School came into being in 1828 as the direct result of the 'great Winchester fagging row'. 'The new institution is a legitimate produce of the disgust universally entertained for the absurdities of the old ones.' It survived to become a public (day) school in its turn, due perhaps to the element of semi-public support, its central position both geographical and academic, its progressive curriculum and methods and its ideological insulation, and the advantage it offered to boys of entering the College as second-year students, some proceeding then to Oxford or Cambridge [66]. On the other hand Bruce Castle, Tottenham, opened in 1827 as a branch of the famous school of the Hill family at Hazlewood in Birmingham, in spite of the enthusiastic support of Bentham and his circle, of its interesting curriculum and experiments in organization and discipline, never became more than quite a small private school. In 1872 it was advertized as preparing for

Fig 4 Bruce Castle, Tottenham, in 1840. (From William Robinson, *History and Antiquities of the Parish of Tottenham*, Volume I.)

'the Universities, Learned Professions and Commercial pursuits'. In 1891 it closed [67].

Topographical research therefore produced ample evidence of the importance, the crucial importance, of private schooling, servicing society and economy at many levels through several rather different periods each with its own special characteristics, and in its final phase both servicing and reinforcing the structure of Professor Perkin's 'viable class society'. But this research also produced evidence that they were not by the reign of Victoria doing it adequately. Their economics were unsound and education as a business in the open market gradually came into conflict with education as a professional skill and concern [68]. Only the more expensive schools could pay assistant masters adequately, and these priced themselves out of the market and were also in the later part of the period especially vulnerable to competition from the new style public schools. Little Philistines whose parents were unable or unwilling to turn them into little Barbarians were already, by the period of the Taunton Inquiry, in real difficulties.

IV

Even before Victoria was on the throne this was realized, and by the forties the 'middle class schools' question was spoken of as a national concern. The *Daily News* in 1847 suggested that the clergy should undertake this important patriotic duty [69]. Studying suburban education with some closeness and intensity made it clear that they had in fact already done so and that throughout the reign of Victoria their professional concern and growing expertise in what today we might call sociological knowledge, in rapidly changing suburban parishes, enabled the clergy to discern new needs and to find the necessary collaborators, both lay and professional, for meeting them. This research did strongly suggest that the earliest and most effective response to an unprecedented demand for new types of education came from the clergy and laity of the established Church. A similar response by other Churches was important, but mainly for children of their own members. Only some examples can be given here to support this statement.

1. The creation of a network of proprietary schools began in 1792 with the foundation of the Philological School in Marylebone. This sprang from a dilettante society with strong Evangelical connections.

Fig 5 The Philological School, New Road, Marylebone. The new building opened
in 1857. (From *The Builder*, 17 October 1857.)

In 1828 the Western Grammar School in Brompton was founded and was able to profit from this early experiment with proprietary standing — investment by proprietors in such an unprofitable concern as education under the rather crude company law of the early nineteenth century had created problems, especially when charitable and proprietary status were still somewhat confused [70]. Then in 1830-1 the founding of a proprietary school in connection with King's College (University College already had such a school) [71] and of a spate of such schools in Middlesex parishes produced the first attempt at a system of secondary schooling.

Meetings of clergy and laity in parishes and districts such as Hackney, Stepney, Islington (where two schools were founded), Kensington, St Peter's Eaton Square, Pimlico, Blackheath (if I may cross the river) between 1830 and 1833 formed schools 'in union with King's College', where their boys could enter as second-year students. These became flourishing and large schools under clerical headmasters, with good assistant staff, some also in Holy Orders, offering a wide curriculum, classics, modern languages, mathematics, science, English, etc. Evidence showed that parents valued this as it opened the universities to their boys as well as a wide range of professional and business opportunities, at a price they could afford, from a staff in which they could have confidence, and in day schools where they could remain in charge of their sons' moral education. Religious instruction was Anglican but does not appear to have been of a proseletyzing kind and many non-Anglican boys attended. One example will suggest the quality and influence of these large and important schools. The second headmaster of the Islington Proprietary School — from 1836 to 1853 — was John Jackson, himself educated under Dr Valpy at Reading, who became in turn Bishop of Lincoln and of London. One of his pupils at Islington was J.L. Brereton who went on to Rugby and then Oxford and later did important work for middle-class education in the West Country [72].

Research into such proprietary schools in this area suggested the need to modify the rather widespread generalization about their belonging to and reinforcing the public-school sector of nineteenth-century education. Certainly schools such as Marlborough, Clifton, Cheltenham, etc., *did* develop into public schools — but in this urban area they did not do so (with the exception of University College School and King's College School now at Wimbledon). They met a distinct and urgent need which coincided in most cases with the reign of Victoria and declined and came to an end when competition from the local reformed endowed schools and the emerging secondary-school system fulfilled that need. In Middlesex certainly they left the ground un-encumbered with institutions that had outlived their use. For this reason it is extraordinarily difficult to find adequate evidence about them. They illustrate the historian's well known temptation to concen-trate on the successes rather than the apparent failures of history — success being measured usually by sheer survival [73].

2. A second systematic attempt by the Church of England to provide for middle-class education was less successful, even in its own day, probably partly because it lacked the secure base of local demand and response which created, sustained and in the end got rid of the proprietary schools.

In 1838 the Bishops of London and Winchester discussed the problem of improving the education of the middle classes in the Metropolis, and any difficulties about using the National Society's funds for this purpose were disposed of satisfactorily. A Metropolitan Schools' Institution was launched to form or aid Middle or Commercial Schools. A central school was established in Rose Street, Soho, to accommodate 250 boys, with a clerical headmaster, a lay under-master and other specialist visiting staff for, for example, French and music. This school was also to train teachers for other schools either estab-lished by the Institution or taken 'into union' with it. By this time the setting-up of the Diocesan Boards of Education made a separate organization unnecessary and the work of the Institution was merged into that of the London Board. An interesting school which took part in this scheme was the East Islington Commercial School, opened in 1841 to fill the gap for the education of the 'intermediate classes, comprising a large amount of the respectability and intelligence of the community'. It taught the truths and duties of Christianity according to the doctrines of the Church of England, English grammatically, Latin, writing, arithmetic and the elements of mathematics, history ancient and modern, geography and chronology, the elements of natural history and philosophy, for 25s. a quarter, and French and drawing for an extra 5s. each [74].

Pressures on the National Society from other sectors of education, especially the need to establish training colleges, or perhaps lack of local response, made this attempt disappointing. From 1841 to 1867 there was little advance, but in 1866 the Society was again concerned with its failure to help the children of the upper labouring and lower middle classes, which were about to be entrusted 'with a large amount of political power and a considerable control over the poorer classes now apparently to be enfranchised' [75]. In 1869 a Middle Class Schools Committee was set up, and began to make grants to such schools, the greater number 'in and about the Metropolis'. But once again, a crisis in elementary education advised caution, and while waiting for the outcome of the Endowed Schools Commission the Middle Class Schools Committee was unable to make much progress [76].

3. Systematic and centralized attempts were in fact far less successful than soundly based local enterprise. For example, in the rapidly developing and socially diversified St Pancras and Camden Town districts keen discernment of pastoral needs enabled the Rev. David Laing and Canon T. Dale to make remarkable contributions to the history of education, national as well as local. It was from Laing's concern for the plight of governesses that the Governesses' Benevolent Institution emerged in 1843, and this in turn developed into Queen's College, Harley Street, for the higher secondary education of 'young ladies above the age of twelve years'. This was the spearhead of the reform of women's education [77]. It was at a parish meeting called in 1850 by Laing's colleague, Canon Thomas Dale, to discuss the problem of middle-class education that the North London Collegiate School for Boys, a private school under the headship of one of his curates, was founded. Throughout the reign of Victoria this provided a sound general education for many hundreds of boys at a charge of nine guineas a year [78]. More important, however, that same meeting inspired Miss Frances Mary Buss to found the North London Collegiate School for Ladies, which became the prototype of the later girls' high schools. This was a purely private venture, but the parish clergy took a kindly interest and visited to teach scripture [79]. Another parish priest who made a notable contribution to the cause of girls' education was Francis Holland, minister of the Quebec Street Chapel, now the Church of the Ascension, Marble Arch. Mrs Holland discerned the need while parish visiting, and her husband during confirmation classes. The two schools in Baker Street (1877) and Graham Street were the result of their formation of the Church of England High Schools Limited Company [80].

My favourite example of parish enterprise is the work of that breezy and indomitable cleric 'Hang Theology Rogers' (1819-96). He became that lowest form of Victorian clerical life, a perpetual curate, when he was presented to the St Thomas Charterhouse district in 1845 — a crowded, pestilential, disreputable area, the overspill of the City through its Newgate, Aldersgate and Ludgate. He called it 'Costermongria' and turned it into a network of schools, including as well as the usual infant and elementary schools a genuine 'middle-class' school and boys' and girls' schools which were 'National Schools of a superior kind', and he even contemplated 'a voluntary class for Greek'. In spite of substantial success in obtaining public grants he had to mortgage his rather meagre private fortune, dun all his friends and evolve startling fund-raising techniques. He was supported and encouraged by men of the stature of William Ellis and F.D. Maurice but his work in his Costermongria reveals very clearly the isolated professionalism of the parish clergy in this respect. They were in the educational front line, Coleridge's clerisy in action, and in this case, and I suspect in more than we realize, it was not sectarian rivalry for the non-existent adherence of the 'lower orders', but professional involvement which gave an impression of, or created, denominational jealousy. Most of us have all too much experience of this in action in our professions. Not that there was anything sectarian or jealous about this particular professional.

In 1858 Rogers was appointed one of the Newcastle Commissioners, and his concern with popular or elementary education continued when he was said to have helped his friend W.E. Forster to draft the Education Bill of 1870 and when a year later he was elected top of the poll as one of the City members on the London School Board. But by this time he had been translated to fairer grounds and had developed new educational interests. He had been made a Canon of St Paul's and a year later in 1863 was presented to the Rectory of St Botolph's-without-Bishopsgate. Here, as he told the Taunton Commission:

> When I moved to Bishopsgate I found that I had more to do with the class of people such as clerks and what may be called the lower middle class . . . parents frequently asked me whether I was going to adopt any steps for establishing middle-class schools. The more I enquired into the matter the more I found that there was a great demand for that sort of school . . . [81]

This robust and enterprising man immediately set to work. An attack on the obsolete City charities got no response, but the City Corporation, recognizing its own needs for adequately educated clerks, bookkeepers, etc., came forward with some funds for a Middle Class Schools

Corporation. This provided what Rogers called 'the plant' for the Cowper Street Middle Class Schools (near Old Street Station). It was during this fund-raising campaign that Rogers earned his nickname. Faced with bickerings about religious instruction and convinced as he was that the parents of the boys already filled the churches and chapels, he was overheard to remark, 'Hang economy, hang theology, let us begin.' [82]

The schools provided a broad general education for boys expected to leave at fifteen or sixteen and to 'take an active share in the Commercial life of London'. Neither Latin nor Greek was part of the staple diet but they were provided for boys who wanted them. The large and austere buildings immediately filled with 700 boys, and the numbers quickly rose to 1,000 and even to 1,200 – but then the cellars had to be fitted up as classrooms. Here for about four guineas a year boys received an education 'not much inferior to that of the sons of gentlemen for which £100 or £150 is usually paid'. These schools had to be self-supporting as all the running expenses had to be met from the fees, and Rogers himself was pleased when the growth of elementary education, the reform of the endowed schools and the emergence of newer forms of secondary education made the Central Foundation Schools, as they became, less necessary. He secured some little endowment for them, the Charity Commissioners provided them with a scheme of government, they 'entered into union' with the Science and Art Department and the Technical Education Board of the L.C.C., and in 1902 quietly, usefully and painlessly became part of the educational apparatus of the new L.E.A. [83].

Rogers's contribution to the middle-class education question had therefore been substantial. But it is rarely acknowledged. It is particularly interesting to encounter the criticisms made of him by Leach in the Victoria County History of Surrey's history of Dulwich College. Rogers in 1857 had been put in charge of reforming Alleyn's College of Gods Gift in Dulwich – his Charterhouse district contained the site of Alleyn's Theatre (one of its few profitable areas because of the vices that flourished there) and boys from his second parish, St Botolph's, were amongst those entitled to education at the free school of the foundation. It was by the mid-nineteenth century one of the more chaotic and ineffectual of the ancient charities and with great exertions and against much opposition Rogers managed to get some of its funds made useful to city boys by endowing the Central Foundation Schools, some of the money used to help in the founding of a girls' high school in Dulwich (the James Allen's Girls' School) and the rest used for reformed almshouses and two boys' schools -- one for Fearon's 'first grade' of pupil, the other more of a second-grade type – Dulwich College and Alleyn's School. Rogers hoped that Dulwich College would serve a wide social range and teach sciences as well or as much as classics. But the College fell into the hands of a powerful headmaster with public-school aspirations and in spite of Rogers's efforts this is what it became, 'giving the same kind of education and school atmosphere that the richer members of the same classes obtain by sending their sons out of town'. In his history Leach accuses Rogers of trying to advance the views of his own parish and of regarding 'all social and therefore educational strata below the level of Eton and above that of the Board School as of one dead level of mediocrity in intellect and culture' [84].

It was an extraordinary assessment of a man who had certainly been at Eton long ago, but whose obituary notices only a few years before Leach was writing had been full of his work for education, especially at varied middle-class levels, and also his work in founding the Bishopsgate Institute to add to the cultural amenities of his City parish. This last example of the Anglican contribution to the middle-class school problem also represents another advantage of local or topographical researches. Who were the 'great figures' in the history of education? Our conventional collection of portraits of the 'great educators' perhaps needs some elaboration.

V

Another aspect of educational history on which much light was thrown by a topographical approach was the history of girls' education. The London suburbs had long provided an almost specialized service in its older traditions and they also provided the necessary meeting place, varied needs and opportunities, the stimulus of a constantly expanding labour market, and the necessary sympathetic and informed male support, for its transformation [85]. But this is too vast a subject to be developed here.

VI

It is difficult to summarize the significance of such research. The crowded, shifting suburban scene drove home the lack of inevitability in historical development – so often implied if not explicitly accepted by historians. By the later nineteenth century the complexity and diversity of expedient, experiment, tradition, etc. etc., made it possible to support from suburban experience almost all the contradictory arguments put forward to the Bryce Commission (1895) for the organization and provision of secondary education. For example, the private sector clearly had much to contribute but was firmly excluded from any participation in the new State system [86]. Perhaps we too readily accept what did happen as both inevitable and as better than what might have happened? It is certainly unfashionable to emphasize the possibilities or achievements of free enterprise in education, but without them topographical research emphasized the impossibility of succeeding in what Dr David Thomson called 'The Victorian Adventure" – the daring experiment of fitting industrial man into a democratic society' [87].

Notes

Acknowledgements are due to the London Borough of Islington for Fig. 1, Cambridge University Press for Fig. 2, Hillingdon Borough Libraries for Fig. 3, the London Borough of Haringey for Fig. 4, and *The Builder* for Fig. 5.

1   V.C.H. *Middlesex*, Vol. 1 (Oxford University Press, for the University of London Institute of Historical Research, 1969), pp. 241-89.
2   See above pp. 1-36.
3   V.C.H. *Middlesex*, Vol. I, pp. 213-40.
4   Ibid. pp. 315-44.
5   V.H. Galbraith, *Introduction to the Use of the Public Records* (Oxford, 1952), p. 12.
6   D. Lysons, *The Environs of London, Being an Historical Account of the Towns, Villages and Hamlets, within Twelve Miles of that Capital* (1792-6), Vol. III, p. 299; Vol. II, pp. 305, 477, 480.
7   E.W. Brayley, *London and Middlesex*, Vol. IV, p. 216.
8   J. Thorne; *Handbook to the Environs of London* (1876; repr. Bath, 1970), Vol. I, p. 217.
9   e.g. *Abstract of Answers and Returns Relative to the State of Education in England and Wales*, pp. 592-4, B.P.P. 1835 (62), xlii.
10   B.P.P. 1834 (572), ix, 1; 1835 (465), vii, 763.
11   *Census of Great Britain 1851 – Education: Report and Tables*, pp. xiii-xx, xxxviii, cii-cliii, 4, 8; B.P.P. 1852-3 (1692), xl, 1.
12   *Royal Commission on the State of Popular Education in England,*

Vol. III. *Reports on Education in the Metropolis and Other Districts,* Pt III, pp. 321, 380, 411-46, B.P.P. 1861 (2794-III), xxi, Pt III.
13 *Schools Inquiry Commission,* Vol. VII, *General Reports on Southern Counties,* B.P.P. 1867-8 (3966-VI), xxviii, Pt VI, p. 233.
14 B.P.P. 1897 (C 8634), lxx, 557.
15 C. Booth, *Life and Labour of the People of London* (1890), 1st ser., *Poverty,* iii.
16 B.P.P. 1895 (C 7862), xliii, 1.
17 B.P.P. 1890-1 (335), xvii.
18 B.P.P. 1908 [Cd. 4374].
19 Board of Education, *Special Reports on Educational Subjects,* Vol. 6, *Preparatory Schools for Boys: Their Place in English Secondary Education* (London, 1900), pp. 79-90, 43.
20 G.B. Hill (ed.), *The Life of Johnson* (Oxford, 1887), e.g. I, p. 46, II, p. 171, 494.
21 Shirley C. Gordon, 'Demands for Education for Girls, 1790-1865' (London Univ. M.A. Thesis, 1950); Mary Rosalie Glyn Grylls, *Queen's College 1848-1948* (London, 1948); *Schools Inquiry Commission,* Pt VI, 1867-8, pp. 580-7, 602 [3966-VI], Pt IV, 1867-8, pp. 697 ff. [3966-IV]; Dame Margaret Janson Tuke, *A History of Bedford College for Women 1849-1937* (London, 1939).
22 *D.N.B.* Woodward; P. Bliss (ed.), *Athenae Oxonienses* (London, 1813-20), III, pp. 1034-5.
23 *D.N.B.* Ainsworth; J. Nichols, *Literary Anecdotes of the Eighteenth Century* (London, 1812-15), V, pp.248-54; Lysons, op. cit. II, p.32; *Notes and Queries,* 6th ser., VII, pp. 64-5.
24 Irene Parker, *Dissenting Academies in England* (Cambridge, 1914), p. 141; H. McLachlan, *English Education under the Test Acts* (Manchester, 1931), p. 9; Wilson, *History and Antiquities of Dissenting Churches,* 4 vols (London, 1808), IV, p. 164.
25 e.g. J.W. Ashley Smith, *The Birth of Modern Education* (London, 1954), pp. 152.
26 N.A. Hans, *New Trends in Education in the Eighteenth Century* (London, 1951), pp. 67, 68-9, 87-91; *D.N.B.* Barrow, Tremamondo; E. Greenberg, 'Contribution to Education of Private Schools in the First Half of the Nineteenth Century' (London Univ. M.A. Thesis, 1953), p. 22.
27 Greenberg, op. cit., esp. pp. 79 ff., 160-4.
28 J. Nelson, *History, Topography and Antiquities of the Parish of St Mary, Islington* (London, 1811), p. 354; *D.N.B.* Edward Miall; Greenberg, op. cit., esp. pp. 164-71.
29 Nelson, op. cit. p. 52; S. Lewis, *History and Topography of the Parish of St Mary, Islington* (London, 1842), p. 349; Greenberg, op. cit. pp. 29, 83-4, 137; *D.N.B.* Evans; *The Times,* 3 January 1821.
30 There are, of course, many exceptions to this generalization, e.g.

Professor Brian Simon, *Studies on the History of Education* (London, 1960).

31   Greater London Record Office, Records of Diocese of London, Vicars General, Books 1520-1685.

32   See above, pp. 83-98, for John Lawson's valuable discussion of this evidence.

33   *Fifty Years of Progress in Education,* 'A Review of the Work of the College of Preceptors, 1846-1896', published by the College; *Schools Inquiry Commission,* Pt III 1867-8, pp. 3-4. [3966-III] ; G. Baron, 'The Secondary Schoolmaster 1895-1914' (unpublished Ph.D. Thesis, Univ. of London, 1952), pp. 433-4.

34   V.C.H. *Middlesex,* I, p. 257.

35   Mary C.E. Chambers, *Life of Mary Ward, 1585-1645,* ed. H.J. Coleridge (1882), *passim;* A.C.F. Beales, *Education Under Penalty* (London, 1963), pp. 98, 103, 203-5, 226-7; Mary D.R. Leys, *Catholics in England 1559-1829* (London, 1961), p. 166; Lysons, op. cit. II, pp. 420-1; T. Faulkner, *Historical and Topographical Account of Fulham* (London, 1813), pp. 343-5; *The Laity's Directory* (1835-6); *Catholic Directory* (1854, 1865).

36   Parker, op. cit. pp. 51, 57-63, 138; McLachlan, op. cit. pp. 2, 10-11, 24, 76-80; Ashley Smith, op. cit. pp. 9-10, 56-61; Nelson, op. cit. pp. 116, 174; Lewis, op. cit. pp. 267-70, 314-15; 319; *D.N.B.* Charles Morton.

37   V.C.H. *Middlesex,* I, pp. 249-51.

38   W.K. Jordan, *Charities of London, 1480-1660* (London, 1960), pp. 208, 210, 219.

39   V.C.H. *Middlesex,* I, p. 242; Foster Watson, 'Notes on Materials on Religious Refugees in their Relation to Education in England', *Proceedings of the Huguenot Society of London for 1909-11* (1911), ix, pp. 80-1, 150; K. Lambley, *Teaching and Cultivation of the French Language, in England during Tudor and Stuart Times* (Manchester and London, 1920), pp. 299 ff.

40   Ambrose Heal, *The English Writing Masters and their Copy-Books* (Cambridge, 1931), pp. 67-8.

41   *D.N.B.* Philip Yorke, William Jones; Hans, op. cit. p. 112; *D.N.B.* Bonnycastle.

42   Chelsea Public Library Local Collection; T. Faulkner, *An Historical and Topographical Description of Chelsea and its Environs* (London, 1810), p. 210; *D.N.B.* ix, p. 124; J. Bettesworth, *Arithmetic Made Easy* (London, 1780), and (with H. Fox) *Observations on Education in General but particularly on Naval Education with a Plan for a Naval Academy* (London, 1782).

43   Hans, op. cit. pp. 67, 103-4; Lysons, op. cit. II, p. 125; Faulkner, *Chelsea,* pp. 334-5; Lewis Lochée, *Essay on Military Education* (London, 1773).

44   Heal, op. cit. p. 112; *D.N.B.* Watts; Hans, op. cit. p. 22.

45   Frances Purton Verney and Margaret Verney, *Memoirs of the Verney Family,* Vol. II (London, 1970), pp. 89-97; Lambley, op.

cit. p. 300; A. Browning (ed.), *Memoirs of Sir John Reresby* (Glasgow, 1936), p. 2; Pepys, *Diary*, 17 January 1660; Thorne, op. cit. II, p. 631; *D.N.B.*

46 R. Parkinson (ed.), for the Chetham Society, *The Autobiography of Henry Newcome*, M.A. (Manchester: Chetham Society, XXVI, XXVII, 1852); Hans, op. cit. pp. 70-6; William Robinson, *Hackney* (London, 1842), p. 140; *Gentleman's Magazine* (1842), N.S. xvii, i, pp. 667-8; (1851), N.S. i, pp. 198-200; Greenberg, op. cit. p. 210; *D.N.B.*, for references see V.C.H. *Middlesex*, I, p. 243, footnote 17.

47 e.g. F. Musgrove, 'The Decline of the Educative Family', *Universities Quarterly* (1960), 14; 'Two Educational Controversies in Eighteenth-Century England', *Paedagogica Historica* (1962), 2.

48 G. Clinch, *Marylebone and St Pancras* (London, 1890), pp. 7, 98; *D.N.B.* John Trusler; W.H. Manchée, 'Marylebone and its Huguenot Associations', *Proc. Hug. Soc.*, XI, No. 1, 65-6; John Gore (ed.), *The Creevey Papers* (London, 1963), pp. 2, 262-5.

49 Harold Perkin, *Origins of Modern English Society 1780-1880* (London, 1969), esp. sections vi-ix.

50 G.R.S. Kitson Clark, *The Making of Victorian England* (London, 1965), pp. 34-42; *The Expanding Society* (Cambridge, 1967), p. 17.

51 John Harkin Best, 'The Academy Keeper, A Dimension in the History of Education', *History of Education Quarterly*, VIII, 3 (Fall 1968).

52 Hans, op. cit. p. 111; *D.N.B.* S. Raffles; Greenberg, op. cit. p. 27; *The Times*, 3 January, 11 December 1821, 12 September 1822.

53 Greenberg, op. cit. pp. 126, 207; *The Times*, 13 January 1821.

54 Islington Public Library Local Collection, YA 160 COL; Greenberg, op. cit. pp. 44, 139, 151; *Morning Herald*, 15 July 1826.

55 Islington Public Library Local Collection, YA 166 MAN; Greenberg, op. cit. p. 150; *Morning Herald*, 1 January 1835; *Morning Chronicle*, 18 July 1836.

56 Patrick Scott, 'The Private School in the Eighteen-Sixties', *History of Education Society Bulletin*, No. 8 (Autumn 1971), pp. 13-25.

57 G.W. Sturges, *The Schools of Edmonton Hundred* (privately printed, 1949), p. 81.

58 See above, p. 102. G.B. Whittaker, *The Boarding School and London Master's Directory* (1828), pp. iv-vi;

59 See above, p. 102.

60 V.C.H. *Middlesex*, I, p. 270.

61 *Crockford's Scholastic Directory* (1861), p. xiii; F.S. de Carteret-Bisson, *Our Schools and Colleges* (London, 1872), p. 275.

62 Ibid. p. 271.

63 Bisson, *Our Schools and Colleges*, 4th ed. (London, 1879), p. 710.

64   *Schools Inquiry Commission*, Pt VI (1867-8), pp. 233-4, 348-9;
      Pt 1, p. 3; Pt III, pp. 3-5, 492; Pt IV, pp. 1 ff., 38.
65   V.C.H. *Middlesex*, 1, pp. 284-5.
66   *Westminster Review*, January 1829, pp. 244-8, quot. E.C. Mack,
      Public Schools and British Opinion, I, p. 159; *Schools Inquiry
      Commission*, Pt III, pp. 313-29; Bisson, *Our Schools and Colleges*
      (1879), p. 763; *Bryce Commission*, 1895, p. 218 (C 7862-I), xliv,
      evidence of H.W. Eve, Headmaster.
67   *D.N.B.* T.W. Hill, Rowland Hill; *Public Education, Plans for the
      Government and Liberal Instruction of Boys in Large Numbers*
      (1822); *Plans for the Government of Hazlewood School* (1825);
      Edinburgh Review, January 1825, Vol. XLI, No. 82, pp. 41, 315;
      A.T. Milne, *Catalogue of the Manuscripts of Jeremy Bentham in
      the Library of University College, London*, Box XVIII, 178-82;
      W. Robinson, *History and Antiquities of the Parish of Tottenham*
      (Tottenham, 1818), pp. 219-20; *Schools Inquiry Commission*,
      Pt IV, pp. 838 ff; Tottenham Museum (Bruce Castle) Local
      Collection; R.L. Archer, *Secondary Education in the Nineteenth
      Century* (Cambridge, 1921), pp. 90 ff.; Sturges, op. cit. p. 71;
      Bisson, *Our Schools* (1872), p. 272; *Our Schools* (1879), p. 885.
68   V.C.H. *Middlesex*, 1, pp. 276-9.
69   *English Journal of Education*, i, pp. 250-4.
70   *Schools Inquiry Commission*, Pt VI (1867-8), pp. 347-8; *Report
      of the Philological School, or School of General Instruction*
      (1834); P. Wayne, *The Philological School or St Marylebone
      Grammar School Past and Present* (privately printed, 1953).
71   See above, p. 120.
72   *Quarterly Journal of Education*, i, pp. 199-203, iv, pp. 183-4;
      Schools Inquiry Commission, Pt IV (1867-8), pp. 340-2, Pt III
      (1867-8), p. 162; Bisson, *Our Schools* (1872), pp. 289, 307; *Our
      Schools* (1879) pp. 765-9; F.J.C. Hearnshaw, *History of King's
      College* (London, 1929), pp. 80-2, 101-4; Kensington Public
      Library Local Collection; Islington Public Library Local Collec-
      tion; Rev. John Owen Parr, *Address at the Opening of the
      Islington School; Rules and Regulations for the Government of
      . . . the Islington Proprietary School; Two Annual Reports . . .
      1830-2; D.N.B.* John Jackson, Joseph Brereton.
73   V.C.H. *Middlesex*, I, pp. 259-60.
74   National Society, 28th Report, 1839, pp. 84 ff., Appendix VI;
      29th Report, pp. 2-7, 22-3; 1st Report of the Metropolitan
      Commercial Schools' Institution, General Committee Minutes
      No. 4, January 1838-July 1847; 2nd Report of the London
      Diocesan Board of Education, July 1841, p. 330; Lewis, op. cit.
      p. 330.
75   National Society, Annual Report 1867. p. 11.
76   National Society, Annual Report 1867, pp. 11-12; 1869, pp. 29-
      35, 17; 1870, pp. 22 ff; 1871, pp. 16-17.
77   V.C.H. *Middlesex*, I, pp. 263, 311-12.

78   *Schools Inquiry Commission*, Pt III (1867-8), pp. 488-563;
      Crockford's Scholastic Directory (1861), xiii; Bisson, *Our Schools*
      (1872), p. 273; F. Boase, *Modern English Biography* (London,
      1965), vi, art. W.C. Williams; *Scholastic World*, 1 August 1878;
      S. Palmer, *St Pancras* (London, 1870), p. 142.
79   V.C.H. *Middlesex*, I, pp. 264, 308-10; *Schools Inquiry Commis-
      sion*, Pt IV (1867-8), pp. 252 ff; Sara A. Burstall, *Frances Mary
      Buss* (London, 1950), *passim*; R.M. Scrimgeour, *N. London
      Collegiate School* (London, 1950), esp. pp. 27-31, 32-4; Gordon,
      op. cit. p. 365; Josephine Kamm, *How Different from Us*
      (London, 1968), *passim*.
80   E. Moberley Bell, *The Francis Holland School* (London, 1938);
      Bisson, *Our Schools and Colleges*, Vol. II: *For Girls* (London,
      1884), p. 439.
81   *Schools Inquiry Commission*, Pt IV (1867-8), pp. 472-81.
82   *The Times*, 20 January 1896.
83   *D.N.B.*; Hadden (ed.), *Reminiscences of William Rogers; Schol-
      astic World*, 1 July 1878, 1 April 1879; *Academia*, 7 March 1868;
      Bisson, *Our Schools* (1872), pp. 265-7; *Our Schools* (1879),
      p. 704; cuttings in collection at Bishopsgate Institute.
84   V.C.H. *Surrey*, II, pp. 198-210.
85   V.C.H. *Middlesex*, I, pp. 263-9.
86   Ibid. pp. 282-4.
87   D. Thomson, *England in the Nineteenth Century*, Pelican History
      of England, No. 8 (Harmondsworth, 1950), pp. 32-3.

GORDON R. BATHO

Sources for the history of history teaching in elementary schools 1833-1914

The outlines of the development of history teaching in elementary schools from the Treasury grants to the National and British and Foreign School Societies in 1833 to the outbreak of the First World War are well established. Direct central control of the school curriculum did not come about until the introduction of the Revised Code in 1862, but parliamentary papers provide extensive evidence of both the intentions and the effects of governmental policy and practice throughout the period. A wide range of other sources, formal and informal, official and private, national and local, supplement our knowledge of how history was being taught in the period and serve as salutary reminders of variation of practice and of the antiquity of some approaches which we too often assume to be exclusive to our own times.

The history of history teaching is a dreary enough story. In securing for every child 'that education, without which life itself is a doubtful blessing', as Sir James Kay-Shuttleworth put it in his *Memorandum on Popular Education* in 1868, 'the Government commenced its work timidly, and continued it feebly for several years' [1]. The early grants were exclusively for the erection of schools and no payments to promote efficiency of instruction were made until 1846. Thereafter, direct encouragement was given to the creation of a more skilful teaching force, and in the succeeding sixteen years the grants of the Committee of Council amounted to an average of approximately one-third of the local expenditure on building and maintaining elementary schools. The teaching of history, the Newcastle Commission of 1858-61 was told by the Rev. James Fraser (later Bishop of Manchester), one of its ten Assistant Commissioners appointed to investigate educational provision, was 'little more than nominal', amounting largely to 'a knowledge of the sequence of the kings and a very slight outline of the general course of events', and in Wales it was commonly 'taught by catechism . . . got up by rote, with the certainty of being forgotten in a day or two' [2] .

The Newcastle Report made recommendations designed to achieve five objects: the application of the existing system of grants to the poorer no less than to the richer districts, the control and regulation of the established level of expenditure, the prevention of any further complication of business in the office of central government, the encouragement of greater local activity and interest in education, and the attainment of a greater measure of elementary knowledge. The Revised Code which followed the Committee of Council's consideration (or alleged consideration) of the recommendations, however, had very different results. The suggestions on the localization of educational administration and for the employment of examiners in addition to inspectors were ignored; the grants for the maintenance of the supply and efficiency of teachers were curtailed; the conditions for the employment of pupil-teachers were so changed that, where the pupil-teacher to child ratio in elementary schools had been 1:36 in 1861, by 1866 it was 1:54 [3] , and a master might have as many as 89 scholars without assistance; and the bulk of the grant was made dependent on the success with which the 3 R's, together with plain needlework for girls, were taught, as measured by an annual examination of each child. In the words of the Board of Education's *Report for 1910-11*, which affords us a survey of the changes in the curriculum of the elementary school from 1833, 'it was not intended that schools should limit their curricula to the three "rudimentary" subjects . . . the purpose of the framers of the Code was to strengthen the lower parts of the existing schools without narrowing or lowering the standard of attainments reached in the higher. But in practice this limitation was undoubtedly produced in the majority of cases' [4] .

It would seem that the introduction of the Revised Code led to the virtual exclusion of history from the timetables, if not always from the teaching, of schools under inspection. Certainly cold comfort is to be derived from the *Report for 1865-6* of the Committee of Council: 'The Revised Code has tended, at least temporarily, to discourage attention to the higher branches of elementary instruction: Geography, Grammar, History. There are signs of recovery, and those schools do best in the elementary subjects where the higher are not neglected' [5] .

Grant-earning considerations largely shaped and determined the curriculum throughout the era of 'payment by results', 1862-95, and until 1890 the teaching of history was not encouraged, although the degree to which it was discouraged varied from one period to another. The Minute of 1867 offered an increased grant to schools which, among other conditions, taught at least one 'specific' subject, such as geography, grammar or history, as well as the 'rudimentary' subjects. The 1871 Code expanded the list of specific subjects, but laid it down that not more than two were to be taken at the same time. In 1872, 71,507 children were examined in one or more of the specific subjects and history, taken by 16,465 children, was the third most popular of the specific subjects, surpassed only by geography, taken by 59,774 children, and grammar, taken by 18,426. By 1875 the number taking history had risen to 17,710, but the increased popularity of English literature reduced the subject's ranking in popularity among the specific subjects to fourth [6].

Under the Code for 1875, the elementary school curriculum was divided into obligatory, class and specific subjects. History figured as one of four class subjects, along with geography, grammar, and plain needlework, of which not more than two could be taken at the same time. Class subjects were to be taught throughout the school above Standard I and to be judged, for a grant of 4s. per child calculated on average attendance, on the proficiency, not of individual children, but of the class as a whole. The list of class subjects was expanded in 1880, but more fundamental changes occurred in 1882. To accommodate the tendency for children to stay longer at school, a seventh standard was introduced, the examination syllabus for which included 'to read a passage from Shakespeare or Milton, or some other standard author, or from a History of England'. On the other hand, the 1882 Code ruled that if any class subjects were taken, one had to be English, and restricted the teaching of history to Standard V and above. By 1890, out of 22,516 departments for older children, English was taught in 20,304 and geography in 12,367, but history was to be found in only 414 [7].

The turning-point for history in the elementary school came with the publication in 1888 of the *Report* of the Cross Commission. Evidence was collected from a limited number of sources and the only individual questioned in depth was an enthusiastic teacher of the subject, W.B. Adams, headmaster of Fleet Road Senior Board School, Hampstead. The Commission's approach was positive, as may be illustrated from the style of the questions posed. Question 14,970 was

'You consider that the study of history tends to quicken the intelligence of the child?'; Question 14,971, 'And you think that the study of history would quicken the love for reading?' [8]. The Cross Commissioners held that the restriction of history to Standard V and upwards had greatly discouraged its systematic teaching and that a syllabus of instruction in the subject should be inserted in the Code. The Code of 1890 carried out these suggestions and removed the rule making English compulsory if any class subject were taken. By 1895, the number of schools taking history rose to 3,597 [9].

1895 marked the end of 'payment by results' and the Code for that year recognized visits to museums as attendances at school 'provided that not more than 20 such attendances may be claimed for any one scholar in the same school year, and that the general arrangements for such visits are submitted for the approval of the inspector' as well as making object lessons, including those on history, compulsory for Standards I, II and III. In 1900, a year after the establishment of the Board of Education, the block grant system was introduced and history was included among the subjects taken 'as a rule' in all schools [10].

History in the elementary school came into its own in many ways between the Balfour Act of 1902 and the outbreak of war in 1914. Where in the 1890s history teaching 'often amounted to very little beyond reading aloud by the children from a text-book, supplemented by incidental questions and explanations from the teacher', direct oral teaching in the subject was undertaken increasingly in the 1900s [11]. The history syllabus also underwent marked changes in the period. At the end of Queen Victoria's reign, the common practice was to teach 'stories chosen on account of their vividness on the one hand and their simplicity on the other' in the classes immediately above the infants, the Tudors in Standard V, the Stuarts in Standard VI and the Hanoverians in Standard VII. In the early 1900s, the 'concentric' method gained popularity in place of this 'periodic' scheme, in an attempt to avoid overloading with details, but by the end of Edward VII's reign many schools were evolving a compromise between the two systems, studying periods in the middle of the elementary school and reviewing the whole course of English history in the top class. Moreover, experiments were taking place in the use of dramatization, the study of local history, and the introduction of lessons on the lives of ordinary people in the past, all aspects emphasized by the interest in 'pageants' which was very marked at the time [12]. In 1905 the Board of Education had discussed and illustrated the teaching of every subject in the curriculum in its significantly entitled volume, *Suggestions to Teachers and Others Concerned in the Work of Public Elementary Schools*, a work which was, and was intended to be, revised from time to time. When in 1923, in its Educational Pamphlet no. 37, it produced a *Report on the Teaching of History*, the section on elementary teaching indicated a further evolution of thinking about the subject. 'History teaching should be, in this early stage, . . . simple, interesting and preliminary; . . . about the end of the twelfth year a first sketch should . . . have been imparted to the scholars of the outstanding figures and events, primarily, but not exclusively, drawn from their own national history. This first connected sketch should, we think, follow on a course of general stories drawn from all countries by which the first interest in history will be inspired' [13] .

The reports of Her Majesty's Inspectors contain a wealth of information about the aims and methods, the extent and content, and the textbooks and reading books available for the practitioners, of history teaching. Indeed, as the Committee of Council commented in a circular letter in 1852, they constituted 'the foundation of the whole system' [14]. The reports were made for educational districts and therefore tend to be general in character, but by cross-reference to a number of districts it is possible to construct from them some overall understanding of what was happening in the teaching of history in schools under inspection. The volume and quality of comment naturally varies from period to period and from H.M.I. to H.M.I. The Rev. H. Moseley, F.R.S., for example, reported on the Birmingham area in 1844 that history was taught to 1,158 children out of 11,982 examined by him, but their knowledge was 'the lowest that could entitle it to the appellation' [15] and on another occasion anticipated a twentieth-century development in the subject by arguing 'it would surely be better to read history backwards' [16] . His colleague Josiah Blandford, also an ordained priest, who was to be an H.M.I. for forty-six years from 1847, displays enthusiasm for integrated studies in his first report: 'For instance, what an excellent lesson in reading, history and geography combined might be given from those stirring lines of Macaulay, in which he describes with such spirit and power, the firing of the beacons announcing the approach of the Spanish Armada . . . I know from experience, that a lesson given on this plan is admirably calculated to keep up the attention of the children' [17] . Again, in 1854, an H.M.I., in listing the attainments of an average boy of twelve in a good school, includes the knowledge of 'the elements of English history' alongside fluency in reading, neat and correct writing from dictation, and the ability to express himself in tolerably correct English, a mastery of the elementary rules of arithmetic and of parsing, and a satisfactory knowledge of geography [18]. After 1862, comment on the teaching of history in H.M.I.s' reports is much more limited.

At first, the reports of H.M.I.s were published in full in the Minutes of the Committee of Council, a principle which the Rev. John Allen, one of the first group of inspectors, firmly established in a dispute with Archbishop Howley and the Lord President the Duke of Buccleuch in 1845, but the growth of Government responsibility brought with it a curtailment of inspectors' freedom. Despite the 'Grand Remonstrance' of 1859 and the resignation of Robert Lowe himself in 1864 after the parliamentary row which resulted from the marking in pencil by the Secretary of the Committee of Council, R.R.W. Lingen, of an H.M.I.'s report, the Select Committee on Education appointed on 12 May 1864 to inquire into the practice with regard to inspectors' reports held that it was correct for the Committee to exercise a supervision and to object to the insertion of irrelevant matter and of controversial argument [19].

H.M.I.s in the nineteenth century almost invariably came from a good-class background, an Oxbridge education (frequently with a religious bias), and had no experience of teaching in public elementary schools. They constituted, therefore, one section of society coming into contact with another which was alien to it, and history teaching was only one small aspect of the work which they were called upon to inspect. It is asking a great deal to expect informed and constructive comment on what could occupy an inspector for a very short time in his visit to a school, itself an occasion which by its very nature limited his opportunity to observe things as they truly were. Even so, some H.M.I.s clearly made an outstanding contribution to the development of history teaching in the period; this is well documented by the reports of the Rev. G.R. Moncrieff in Bristol and of H.E.B. Harrison, later to be Chief Inspector, when he was in Liverpool.

Other inspectors have left us reminiscences which generally prove a refreshing contrast to their official reports. Among H.M.I.s, Sir Joshua Fitch published two collections of lectures, *Lectures on Teaching* (1884), and *Educational Aims and Methods* (1900), and E.G.A. Holmes was a prolific writer, perhaps best known for his *What is and What Might be* (London, 1911). E.M. Sneyd-Kynnersley produced *H.M.I.* in 1908 and A.P. Graves *To Return to All That* (London, 1930). The reminiscences of School Board and local authority inspectors have a particular interest, for from the earliest days they generally had had practical experience in the classroom. Among these the three best-known volumes are probably G.A. Christian's *English Education from Within* (London, 1922), P.B. Ballard's *Things I Cannot Forget* (London, 1937) and F.H. Spencer's *An Inspector's Testament* (London, 1938). As John Leese reminds us in *Personalities and Power in English Education* (Leeds, 1950), the Rev. D.R. Fearon wrote a manual, *School Inspection*, based on his experience as an H.M.I. from 1860 to 1870, and published in 1876, which incidentally gives us a graphic description of the 'inspection day'.

Fearon was a staunch supporter of the Revised Code, maintaining that a grounding in the elements was essential, though he thought that some of the time devoted to geography and grammar might have been better employed in English composition and advanced arithmetic. His ideas on the teaching of history are particularly interesting. He advocated correlation of history and geography, suggesting, for example, that the speeches of Oliver Cromwell and the letters of Thomas Carlyle could illustrate the geography of Ireland. He was keen on the utilization in history teaching of diverse resources and mentions the value of such materials as county histories and Murray's guides. He thought homework essential, to allow factual matter to be learnt in readiness for lessons. 'Nothing will carry the civilizing influence of the school more universally into the houses, into the alleys and street doors, than the requirement of home-lessons. The inspector should always ask at the commencement of a history or geography lesson, "What did you require them to prepare for this lesson?".' He held the learning of salient dates to be fundamentally important. 'Many teachers pooh-pooh dates . . . This doctrine is a consequence of the reaction against the old-fashioned method of teaching history . . . by making the children learn little else than dates. Dates are to the study of history what the multiplication table is to arithmetic. They are an essential framework on which to build up and keep sustained, all the scholar's historical learning' [20] The matter of dates in history teaching, still controversial in the 1970s, was discussed in the 1923 *Report on the Teaching of History* of the Board of Education, and what was then said provides an interesting parallel with Fearon's point of view. The *Report* complains of 'the increasing tendency of late to depreciate the value of the accurate fact and still more of the date in the teaching of History' and calls for 'a deliberate attempt to develop some sense of sequence in History, by giving the children an idea of the main landmarks in History as they stand out on a simple time chart' between the ages of nine and twelve or thirteen, with the learning of twenty or thirty important dates [21].

Probably the only memoir by a late nineteenth-century elementary schoolteacher to survive is James Runciman's *Schools and Scholars* (1887). As Kay-Shuttleworth never forgot, the training of teachers is a vital element in the creation of any education system and Runciman's account of a lesson at 'Russell Street training college for men' is a penetrating indictment of the decline in standards brought about by the Revised Code, which made Kay-Shuttleworth so angry. It is also a fascinating glimpse of contemporary preparation for history teaching in the elementary school and as such deserves quotation here at length:

> The historical tutor entered and began with a resolute monotonous snuffle. 'What happened on September 25, 1066? Hands up those who know.' Then 'men' held up their hands in a childish way . . . The quiet eye of the tutor ran over the benches until it lighted on some unhappy mortal soul who had not held up his hand. A shudder of apprehension thrilled the class. 'Mr Jones.' 'Don't know, Sir.' 'This is very serious Mr Jones. The very first date. Most serious. How long did you devote to the two pages of dates which I set?' 'About an hour, sir. I had a good deal of other work to do.' 'An hour. An hour to the most important period in history! This is simply scandalous, outrageous. It will have a serious effect on your future career, Jones. I shall take a note of the matter in my register.' Then a solemn entry was made and Jones' doom was regarded as sealed. 'Let us pass on. I take the seventh date from the bottom of page 7.' Then the teacher repeated some rigmarole about some battle or other, using the exact words from the little book with one exception. 'I missed one word in reading that paragraph. What was the word I missed?' Again the hands went up and again the luckless fellows with hazy memories came under the threatening eye, the awful finger of Mr Moatt. 'Annesley.' 'I have only a general knowledge of the paragraph, sir.' 'General knowledge! General knowledge, sir! But you must learn the lesson *verbatim*.' . . . The grand list was reserved till the close of the hour. It ran something in this way: 'Write down what happened in 1086, 1084, 1001, 1113, 1139, 1109.' (When the exercise was over the students changed paper and marked someone else's work.) . . . To omit a semicolon was culpable; to leave out a preposition was worse; while to omit the day of the month on which somebody signed something, or killed somebody else, was regarded as next door to criminal. The papers were handed back to the owners . . . [and] the inquisitor proceeded to register results. 'Mr Jones.' 'Four right, sir!' 'That is very bad.' 'Mr Thompson.' 'Six right, sir!' (A grunt of satisfaction.) 'Mr Rutherford.' 'One right, sir.' A dead silence fell on the assembly and each trembling student waited for the thunderbolt. The pregnant pause lasted

during some dread seconds. 'Did I understand you to say one right, Mr Rutherford?' 'That is all, sir.' Another pause. The silence seemed pulsating with tremor of sheer terror. Then came the ferociously grave sentence. 'Mr Rutherford, you need not look for a certificate at the end of your term. Your prospects are – well, I will not particularize.' [22]

Runciman tells us that this kind of experience was repeated three times a week. He adds that the tutor was in fact a sound historical student who fully appreciated the approach which an intelligent teacher should take, but depicts him as the victim of a system. It is easy to realize why Runciman's contemporary at Borough Road Training College from 1871-5, P.B. Ballard, refers to him with evident awe and why G.A. Christian speaks of him as 'the educational comet of the early school board era' [23].

Article 50 of the Revised Code stated that in school log-books 'no reflections or opinions of a general character are to be entered' and references to the teaching of history in such log-books as have survived from the nineteenth and early twentieth centuries tend to be both infrequent and laconic. The paucity of the material available from the source is, however, compensated by its unquestionable authenticity and upon occasion the search for information among manuscripts which are widely scattered is rewarded with a gem. Here, for instance, are some entries in the log-book of East Retford boys' elementary school in 1866-7:

June 19 1866	Gave first class some questions on a chapter of English history which they had read four times.
March 26 1867	First class learned kings of England from William I to Richard III with dates.
April 11 1867	First class read one chapter of English history three times to smaller classes; they read the same twice simultaneously.

History was dropped from the syllabus later in 1867 [24]! Very few children's exercise books have survived and comparatively few pupil-teachers', but these also are invaluable when they are found. Dr C.J. Phillips has told us that the notebook of a student in training in 1856 at the Westminster Training College, Horseferry Road, shows that he was advised to make use in the history lesson of historical pictures, collections of coins, spent bullets, pieces of armour, illustrative documents and models [25]. Again, Harriet Wager's exercise book as a pupil-teacher in 1858, which has found its way into Derbyshire Record

Office, illustrates for us the contemporary passion for mnemonic verses:

> Now comes the Eighth Henry, in royal array,
> The Blue Beard of England, historians say;
> Who, by passion incited, or jealousy led,
> Thought nothing of shortening his wives by a head,
> Divorces and murders astonished the nation,
> The monks lost their cash in the new Reformation,
> Great Cardinal Wolsey was left in the lurch,
> And the king lived and died, 'supreme head of the Church'.

What has survived, of course, is a wide range of school history textbooks and reading books. The Universities of Hull, Leicester, London, Sheffield and Southampton all possess specialized collections of these, and Valerie Chancellor prints an extensive list, classified into books for children below and above thirteen years of age, in her *History for Their Masters* (Bath, 1970). Although upon occasion one cannot but agree with J.R. Green's comment in his *A Short Geography of the British Islands* (1880) that 'no drearier task can be set for the worst of criminals than that of studying a set of text-books such as the children in our schools are doomed to use', textbooks afford us significant insights into the contemporary aims and methods of teaching history and there is no doubt that the influence exerted by them on teaching was vitally important at a time when teachers tended to depend on them very heavily. It is more difficult to assess the significance of any particular textbook. References to textbooks may be found in school log-books or inspectors' reports, but such references prove little other than that a particular book was in use at a particular school in a particular year. No statistics exist on how many books, or even which books, were in use at any particular moment of time. Perhaps the most reliable indication of the general importance of a book may be obtained from the time span in which it was available and from the number of editions through which it passed. Richmal Mangnall (1769-1820), headmistress of Crofton Old Hall, was the author of *Mangnall's Historical Questions*, which was an exceptionally popular schoolroom encyclopedia, first published in 1808, of which the 84th edition was reprinted in America in 1857, and still being reprinted in 1892. Others in a similar bracket of importance were Goldsmith's *History*, Mrs Markham's *History of England* and Lady Callcott's *Little Arthur's History of England*. The historical coverage of Mangnall spans the questions 'What monarchies were first founded after the deluge?' to 'What public acts shed a lustre upon the concluding period of the reign of George the Fourth?' and its period flavour is perhaps adequately illustrated by the answer to the question on the character of the Greeks: 'Glory and liberty were their darling passions; but their liberty frequently degenerated into licentiousness.' But the doyen of stodge, Dr W. Lamont has pointed out, is Henry Ince, whose *Outlines of English History* was in print from 1849 until at least 1906 and sold nearly a quarter of a million copies. From Ince one could learn such uplifting information as that George II's son died from the blow of a cricket ball. The prefaces of textbooks repay study and Ince's is no exception. 'The importance of having the outlines of every study accurately defined, and the leading points and bearings correctly acquired before the *minutiae* are entered into, will be readily conceded; and also that if the groundwork be clearly traced in early life it will scarcely ever be obliterated; but that subsequent reading and even conversation, will continue to supply materials for the completion of the sketch' [26]. It was not only inspectors who tended to be drawn from another social milieu than the elementary school teacher's.

Advice on how to teach history in school was not in short supply in the period, especially in the 1890s and 1900s. Quite apart from a vast periodical literature − for the 1840s and 1850s alone, for instance, one could not ignore *The Edinburgh Review, The Quarterly Journal of Education, The Educational Magazine, The English Journal of Education, The Monthly Paper of the National Society, Quarterly Educational Magazine and Record of the Home and Colonial Society, The Educational Record, Papers for the Schoolmaster, The Educational Expositor* or *The School and the Teacher* − increasing numbers of teaching manuals were being published. From Thomas Tate's *The Philosophy of Education* (1854), for example, the elementary school teacher could learn to draw contrasts between historical characters; Tate's delicious piece on Alfred the Great and Charles II begins by contrasting Alfred as 'The glory of his country. Amid dangers and toil, devoted himself to his country' and Charles as 'A disgrace to humanity. After much bloodshed he became king and then devoted his country to himself.' The standard work, or at any rate one which had an enormous impact in the second half of the nineteenth century, was John Gill's *Introductory Textbook to School Education*. In the eighth edition of 1862, Gill advocated teaching history by the collective lesson and advised the teacher to take three aspects in depth − social, political and religious − dealing with the present day, an earlier period, and then comparing and contrasting the past situation with the modern. 'This method', he commented, 'has a value in quickening children's observations as to the things by which they are surrounded, and leading them to see some importance in the matters of everyday life.' [27] Another, less well-known early manual was the *Handbook on the Teaching and Management of Elementary Schools* (Manchester, c. 1875), by the editor of the *National Schoolmaster*.

The rise of a history teaching profession at the secondary and tertiary levels of education meant that still more advice became available for the elementary school teacher on the nature of the subject and on the problems of teaching it. The Conference on Historical Teaching in Schools, organized by the Royal Historical Society in 1887 and presided over by Bishop Creighton, was 'the largest meeting ever got together for the discussion of an educational question' [28]. Four years later the Council of the Society, on the initiative of its chairman, Oscar Browning, appointed a committee to consider the development of the study of history in schools. The creation of the Historical Association in 1906 was even more significant, for that body immediately launched the publication of pamphlets on the teaching of history as well as on specific historical topics. The authoritative nature of Historical Association pamphlets and pronouncements was rapidly established. There is, for instance, a degree of common thinking displayed in the records of its meeting on local history and the appropriate section of the Board of Education Circular 599 of 1908 which can scarcely be coincidental; the Circular is on the 'Teaching of History in Secondary Schools', but elementary schools must surely have been influenced by the Board's statement in paragraph 7 of the Circular: 'It is essential that in each school attention should be paid to the history of the town and district in which it is situated.' Equally, the devotion of the Historical Association's first pamphlet to a study of 'Sources' by Sir Charles Harding Firth must have reinforced the comment in the Board's *Suggestions for . . . Public Elementary Schools* a year earlier that 'the reading to the class from time to time of striking passages from original authorities . . . will deepen and intensify the effects of a lesson' [29].

As late as 1899 the Committee of Seven of the American Historical Association in its famous report on *The Study of History in Schools* could write about England that 'the most noticeable features are a lack of historical instruction, a common failure to recognize the value of history, and a certain incoherence and general confusion'. In the years immediately prior to the First World War, a lively debate was taking place in this country about the teaching of history at all levels, however, to which important contributions were being made by university teachers in both history and education, by central government and local authority officials, and by schoolteachers themselves. To quote only a few of the galaxy of publications from this period suffices to indicate the range and quality of the debate. 1900 saw the publication of the Board of Education Special Report by A.M. Curteiss on 'The Teaching of History in Preparatory Schools', summarizing with pungent comment the results of a questionnaire to 120 schools [30]. By 1902, H.E. Bourne was warning in his *The Teaching of History and Civics* that the 'source method' could be adopted too enthusiastically; 'the pupils should not be allowed to entertain the flattering notion that they are doing what historians have been obliged to do, except as the infant toddles in the path run by the athlete' [31]. H.L. Withers was reporting to the L.C.C. in 1904: 'It is because of its bearing on the future of our civic and national life, even more than on account of its value to the imagination and the understanding that the study of history may claim an honoured place on the time table of our primary schools.' [32] In his address to the first annual general meeting of the Historical Association at University College, London, on 8 February 1907, James Bryce made a resounding pronouncement on the object of teaching history:

> It is not perhaps going too far to say that the true qualification of the historian consists in this — to be able to see the past as if it was the past; by which I mean, to see the past as it appeared to the people who then lived, to see it with their eyes, to feel it with their feelings, to enter into the sentiments which moved them, to understand their motives, to know what the Germans call their *Weltanschauung*, their idea of the world, their conception of the world and of the relation of men to Nature and the Deity. These are the things which make for reality in history. These are the things in which each age differs from other ages. [33]

In 1910 Wiltshire Education Committee adopted a report on the 'Supply of History Books and the Teaching of History in Elementary Schools' which provided that every child in the upper standards should have his own textbook and that teachers should be supplied with single copies of some standard books of reference and books dealing with particular topics, including material and local history [34]. 'The amount of information a child can retain is small, and efforts to make it extensive are thrown away, but it is most important that a child should realize before he leaves school how his country is governed, what he inherits from the past, and what duties he owes as a patriot and a citizen,' the Wiltshire memorandum stated. It was a sentiment which would have been approved by Miss M.L.V. Hughes, who published her *Citizen To Be* in 1915 and expressed the hope that the elementary-school history syllabus would rid itself of 'the details of remote wars, of court intrigues, of royal pedigrees, of much Constitutional History' [35].

Debate of this intensity and extent clearly indicates a healthy discontent among administrators, theorists and teachers alike. It would be good to know how it all appeared to the recipients of education in the period. Unfortunately, very few memoirs exist by pupils, though it is very much to be hoped that the survivors from the latter part of the period at any rate will be persuaded to record their impressions, if not in writing, then at least on tape. When we do have the testimony of a Joseph Ashby or a Flora Thompson, of course, the overriding impression is of a concentration upon the 3R's — 'Right up the school', Joseph Ashby's daughter tells us in confirmation of all that we know of the effects of the Revised Code, ' . . . you did almost nothing except reading, writing and arithmetic' — and only rarely is there mention of history, as when Flora Thompson reminds us that in the 1880s 'History was not taught formally; but history readers were in use containing such picturesque stories as those of King Alfred and the cakes, King Canute commanding the waves, the loss of the White Ship, and Raleigh spreading his cloak for Queen Elizabeth.' [36]

No agreement had been reached by 1914, or ought to have been, indeed, on how to teach history in the elementary school. This is both the fascination of the art and the difficulty of the student of its practice. But probably all concerned, then as now, would accept the conclusion of the Board of Education *Report for 1910-11*: 'in the long run success or failure in History teaching, more perhaps than in any other subject, depends upon the ability and interest of the individual teacher' [37].

Notes

1   Sir James Kay-Shuttleworth, *Memorandum on Popular Education* (1868, reprinted 1969), p. 7.
2   *Newcastle Commission Report*, Vol. II, pp. 223, 224, 561.

3   Matthew Arnold's General Report for the year 1867, q.
    J.S. Maclure, *Educational Documents England and Wales 1816-
    1968* (London, 1971), p. 81.
4   *Report of the Board of Education for the year 1910-1911*
    (1912), pp. 7-8.
5   *Minutes of the Committee of Council, 1865-6*, p. xiii.
6   *Report of the Board of Education for the year 1910-1911*
    (1912), p. 9.
7   Ibid. pp. 10-14.
8   *Cross Commission Report*, p. 46.
9   *Report of the Board of Education for the year 1910-1911*
    (1912), p. 17.
10 Ibid. pp. 18-19.
11 Ibid. pp. 33-4.
12 Ibid. pp. 34-5.
13 Board of Education Educational Pamphlet no. 37, *Report on the
    Teaching of History* (1923), pp. 11-12.
14 Circular letter of the Committee of Council to H.M.I.s, 1852,
    q. E.L. Edmonds, *The School Inspector* (London, 1962), p. 51.
15 *Minutes of the Committee of Council*, 1845, p. 505.
16 N. Ball, *Her Majesty's Inspectorate 1839-1849* (Birmingham,
    1963), p. 104.
17 Ibid. p. 117.
18 *Report of the Board of Education for the year 1910-1911*
    (1912), pp. 4-5.
19 N. Ball, op. cit. pp. 206-8; E.L. Edmonds, op. cit. pp. 180-3.
20 D.R. Fearon, *School Inspection* (1876), p. 84, q. J. Leese,
    Personalities and Power in English Education (Leeds, 1950),
    p. 136.
21 Board of Education Educational Pamphlet no. 37, *Report on
    the Teaching of History* (1923), pp. 13-14 and Appendix I,
    'A Suggested Alphabet of History'.
22 J. Runciman, *Schools and Scholars* (1887), pp. 142-6.
23 G.A. Christian, *English Education from Within* (London, 1922),
    p. 131.
24 I am indebted for this reference to my Ph.D. student, Mr D.G.
    Williams, of Eaton Hall College of Education.
25 *The Times Educational Supplement* (28 January 1972), p. 86.
26 W. Lamont, 'The Uses and Abuses of Examinations', in M. Ballard
    (ed.), *New Movements in the Study and Teaching of History*
    (London, 1970), pp. 194, 197.
27 J. Gill, *Introductory Textbook in School Education* (eighth
    edition, 1862), p. 148.
28 R.A. Humphreys, *The Royal Historical Society 1868-1968*
    (London, 1969), pp. 21-2.
29 Board of Education, *Suggestions to Teachers and Others Con-
    cerned in the Work of Public Elementary Schools* (1905),
    p. 106.

30 A.M. Curteiss, 'The Teaching of History in Preparatory Schools',
    Board of Education *Special Reports,* Vol. 6 (1900), pp. 207-18.
31 H.E. Bourne, *The Teaching of History and Civics* (New York,
    1902, revised 1915), p. 173.
32 H.L. Withers, *The Teaching of History and Other Papers*
    (Manchester, 1904), p. 200.
33 James Bryce, *On The Teaching of History in Schools,* Leaflet
    no. 4 of the Historical Association (1907).
34 *Minutes* of the Wiltshire Education Committee, 24 June 1910,
    pp. 16-17; I am indebted for this reference to my Ph.D. student,
    Mr I.J.D. Steele, of Madeley College of Education.
35 Miss M.L.V. Hughes, *Citizen To Be* (London, 1915), p. 148.
36 M.K. Ashby, *Joseph Ashby of Tysoe,* 1859-1919 (1961), q.
    P.H.J.H. Gosden, *How They Were Taught* (Oxford, 1969), p. 41;
    Flora Thompson, *Lark Rise, an Oxfordshire Hamlet in the
    'Eighties* (1939), q. P. Teed and M. Clark, *Portraits and
    Documents: Later Nineteenth Century 1868-1919* (London,
    1969), p. 287.
37 *Report of the Board of Education for the year 1910-1911*
    (1912), p. 35.

BOWMAN, F.L. 'The Teaching of History in the Elementary Training
    College and Public Elementary School' M.Ed. Manchester, 1919.

CHANCELLOR, V.E. 'Some Attitudes in School Text Books in English
    History 1800 to 1914' M.Ed. Birmingham, 1967.

DOBSON, J.L. 'A Study of Attitude Among Adolescents Towards
    British History and Institutions' M.Ed. Durham, 1950.

HOLWELL, E.W. 'Some Principles and Practice in the Teaching of
    History in Schools in England in the Eighteenth and Nineteenth
    Centuries' M.Ed. Hull, 1958.

HONEYBONE, M.J. 'The Use of Primary Source Materials in the
    Teaching of History, 1900 to 1970' M.Ed. Birmingham, 1971.

PARTON, J.G. 'The Development of the Teaching of History in
    Schools in England During the Nineteenth and Twentieth Centuries'
    M.Ed. Liverpool, 1966.

PILSBURY, W.A. 'A Consideration of some of the Text Books on
    Modern History Used in Secondary Schools Since 1860' M.A.
    Reading, 1944

NORMAN MORRIS

The contribution of local investigations to historical knowledge

I

Educational historians appear to be agreed that research into local history gives their subject an additional dimension. In a recent review article [1], Margaret Bryant kaleidoscopes a number of reasons for this belief:

> The history of education is in an urgent need of local research to actualize and substantiate its generalizations, its large statements of legislative, administrative or academic intent, and also to investigate the undergrowth of provision of education of widely varied sorts as response to social and personal needs, owing little or nothing to policy at any level but servicing society and the economy, as well as enriching the personal life. If we want to know what did happen rather than what was supposed to be done, we have to go into the field and find out.

This portmanteau statement is a useful starting-point for an examination of the value of local studies which are seen to have three main functions — to enlarge our knowledge of what happened, to put flesh and perhaps clothes on what might otherwise be only a skeletal framework and to provide a correctional coda to the national story.

There is much that is self-evident in each of these points. Nevertheless, they also suggest a number of questions. Before we can assess the value of local sources as a contribution to knowledge we need to understand the nature of local information; is it really just a footnote illustrating or embellishing a central story, or has it a more integral role as a main character in the story? When Miss Bryant tells us that we need to go into the field to find out what 'did happen rather than what was supposed to be done', is she inferring that governmental policy may, on occasions, have pulled one way and local action another, so that we need field information to correct the view which we might derive from use of central sources only? Or, alternatively, is she saying that it is historians who have misunderstood the nature of educational dynamics and that local studies are necessary to adjust perspectives projected not by the makers but by the writers of history? If the latter is the case, we need to examine the nature of what passes as national history and consider what validity there can be in any picture of education, whether at the level of policy formation or simple description, which does not include the localities.

The nature of the evidence available to historians of particular institutions is always, to a considerable extent, a reflection of the nature of the institutions themselves; as institutions develop or change in character, so the amount and type of data thrown up will also probably change. This has clearly happened in the case of education. There is a vast difference, for example, between the material available for the study of schools in the seventeenth and nineteenth centuries: sources and records for the later period are not just more plentiful; they are different in kind. It needs no more than a glance at the published documents of Leach or Sylvester on the one hand, and Maclure on the other, to bring home the point that before 1800 the education question was mainly private and local and that after 1800 it became public and central.

In an earlier paper in this volume Mr Lawson has surveyed sources for a period before 1800 and it is clear that his analysis of local material covers the entire range of information available for building up the national picture in the centuries with which he is dealing. To understand why education was as it was before 1800, to appreciate its aims and the motives of school founders, or to test the efficiency as well as the quantity of education supplied, we are naturally restricted to specific studies of local happening, just because educational activity was sporadic and uncoordinated. National history for that time is of necessity the sum of local studies because the centre of gravity was in the localities. The situation changed, however, when government started to take an interest. From 1800 onwards we begin to have a new and growing body of centrally produced information which is by no means confined to the aspirations, attitudes and actions of Ministers or civil servants; we now have an ever-enlarging repository of officially collected data covering almost every aspect of local educational activity. In this circumstance we are forced to ask what additional contribution to the national picture can be expected from local research. Do we, in fact, need local studies to adjust or supplement the story as told in central archives?

Whenever the State has accepted even tacit responsibility for educational policy it is unlikely that local areas can ever pursue significantly separate paths or promote developments of importance without the knowledge of central government. Cases of direct confrontation, in which a local authority challenges a central directive, are rare; when they do occur they are certainly not unnoticed by Whitehall or Curzon Street. Within a period of fifteen years, Merthyr Tydfil twice refused to conform to national policy − in 1956, when it declined to operate the Government's request to keep physically fit teachers in service beyond the age of sixty-five as a means of combating the problem of teacher shortage, and in 1971 over the issue of school milk for junior children. But in both instances the Government was appraised of the situation and used the threat of legal penalties to enforce compliance. If there is any gain from studying these two episodes in the areas in which they occurred, it is in examining the nature of the local circumstances and the particular forces and pressures which led to Merthyr's demonstrations of independence, as case studies either in local government or in the relationship between central and local government, rather than as examples of local flowerings divorced from central activity.

In dealing with these instances the Government was able to deploy sanctions to keep Merthyr on the national highway. It is possible to imagine other divergencies where the central authority has no legal remedy and the local story really does depart from the national script. It may be thought that when the history of secondary reorganization on comprehensive lines comes to be written it will illustrate the dictum that what takes place locally is not always what the Government wants to happen. The full story will, of course, have to record a number of local differences and even direct refusals by certain local authorities to produce schemes of reorganization; but it would be quite wrong to suppose that these took the Government by surprise or were, in any sense, deviations. Official policy was, in fact, so designed as to take advantage of anticipated local unilateralism. In the absence of any precisely defined power enabling him to order the submission of schemes, the Secretary of State merely 'requested' authorities to prepare them in the expectation (fully justified in the outcome) that whilst some would decline, many others would comply. Implementation of schemes could only be carried out piecemeal over a period of time and it made sense to make a start on the soft under-belly of local areas which were already more than half willing to make the change. Instead of inviting a head-on clash with dissident councils the Government chose a strategy of erosion; at the end of the day, when more and more areas had fallen voluntarily into line and the new principle had become respectable, it would be relatively easy to mop up the hard-core residue. It may well be that future textbook orthodoxy will distort this study into a tale of governmental grand policy which went wrong; local historians may be called in to show that what was supposed to happen did not happen everywhere or at the same time. But to believe that this was contrary to governmental strategy and that local studies will be necessary to put the picture straight is to misrepresent the actual intentions of Circular 10/65 as well as to underrate the political shrewdness of its authors.

Whenever historians record that central policy was frustrated by the refusal of local authorities to co-operate, or that Governments were compelled to modify their attitudes under local pressures, an alarm bell should sound. Adaptation to changing circumstances is a normal political process. It is probable that the Ministry of Education finally and grudgingly abandoned its opposition to public examinations below G.C.E. O-level only because an extremely high proportion of schools were already entering candidates for lower-level examinations and the Ministry had no alternative but to recognise a *de facto* situation. On the other hand, many instances which are usually quoted to illustrate the power of local practice to alter or divert central aims do not stand up to investigation. It has been supposed, for example, that in the first decade of this century teacher opposition successfully blocked efforts of the Board of Education to swing the secondary-school curriculum away from a technical bias and to impose a literary emphasis reflecting the classical upbringing of the upper classes in general and the new Permanent Secretary, Sir Robert Morant, in particular. The story itself has a classical roundness. Morant is supposed to have fired his opening shot in the form of the 1904 Secondary School Regulations and to have spent the following years trying to enforce them. But the schools (so the tale continues) took a broader view and came to the defence of science and the more practical subjects. After a running battle, the Board began to retreat, slowly at first, but more rapidly after Morant's removal from the scene in 1911; the Board put out reluctant peace-feelers in its Annual Report for 1912-13 and was finally routed in 1917 — after years of Liberal rule and near-defeat in a World War had exposed the deficiencies of English education – by the Leathers report on modern studies and the Thomson report on natural sciences. According to this version, the course of history was changed by the struggle of progressive elements in the schools against arch-conservatives at the central office.

Unfortunately, there is little to substantiate this. The evidence, indeed, stands the story on its head. The 1904 Regulations and the mass of circulars, reports and correspondence which followed over the next ten years make quite clear that the Board saw secondary schools as places of *general* education. If they drew attention to the importance of literary subjects it was as part of a balanced curriculum comprising science, mathematics and practical subjects in addition to the arts. Not infrequently it was the Board itself that insisted on the inclusion of handicraft and domestic subjects in secondary schools where teachers conservatively clung to the traditional literary curriculum which was all they knew. From at least the beginning of the century the Board seems to have worked in accordance with two principles – that specific vocational training should be confined to technical institutions, leaving schools as places of general education; and that schools, whether higher elementary or secondary, should provide a curriculum suited to the general needs of the pupils attending them. These could vary from school to school but all subjects had a contribution to make. Thus, within a year of issuing the 1904 Regulations, the Board took Stockport Education Committee to task for the unrealistic and over-literary curriculum of its municipal secondary school:

> . . . in the case of a school in which the school life is relatively short . . . [the Board] attach much importance to the inclusion in the curriculum of an adequate course of manual work because of its general educational value for all the boys . . . While the school should have as one of its objects to turn out boys fully equipped for an industrial career, the claims of manual work in the case of boys who may be destined for commercial occupations are of much educational weight. [2]

Time given to woodwork, practical chemistry and mechanical drawing should be increased and provision made for both physics and chemistry in Forms IIIa and IVa. Five years later H.M.I.s expressed satisfaction with changes which had been made for boys but felt that the girls' curriculum still left much to be desired. Many girls entered teaching or took up office work; there was a residue, however, whose sights were no higher than 'skilled handwork' and for these H.M.I.s strongly urged a course of artistic training through needlework.

It is clear that practice in this school had been at loggerheads with Board policy. But if this local incident has value to the historian it is in showing that whilst teachers had difficulty in developing new concepts of education the Board itself was ready to give a lead. There is a second inference that if this verdict conflicts with a hitherto generally accepted interpretation of Board policy history should be rewritten to take account of it. But it is important to note that the new information which suggests the need for reinterpretation, comes from national, not local, sources. Regulations and circulars concerning the curriculum, H.M.I.s reports on schools and correspondence between the Board and local authorities are national records; so, too, are many of the chief sources from which we derive other field information; much of our knowledge about the local provision and financing of schools in the nineteenth century, for example, comes from school files in the Public Record Office. If we are wrong about central policy on a wide variety of issues, it may not be through lack of adequate local information but because we have failed to read, or have misunderstood, what central documents say.

It is a platitude to say that no two local authorities − or, for that matter, schools − are entirely alike or carry out all their functions in precisely the same way. But if our concern is with trends and the construction of generalizations it is important to remember that since the State began to intervene in education the most accessible and reliable records of field behaviour itself are frequently those compiled and maintained by central agencies and located nationally. This is a direct result of the nature of central authority, and the way in which the national system developed. Instead of superseding local agencies the State chose to work through them. Consequently, although the greater part of educational history continued to take place locally, it was essential to its own purpose for the State to know what was happening; effective intelligence is always a first requisite of government. From their initial appointment, H.M.I.s were the eyes and ears of the central office and it is often astonishing to discover just how much and what sort of information they channelled to London. Throughout the nineteenth century, government developed increasingly sophisticated inquisitional techniques; it is difficult today, for example, to challenge, or reproduce from other sources, the extreme detail which assistant commissioners put into the Clarendon or Taunton reports. Central authority has given itself statutory power to obtain whatever information or returns it requires, and amateurs are rarely in a position to question officially produced evidence. For periods prior to 1800, before the State began to accumulate its own data, the only way of seeing education as a whole is through specific reportage of individual areas and events and stringing them in series. Beyond 1800, a similar jig-saw of isolated snap-shots is not only unnecessary but might give a less complete, and more unreliable picture than can be obtained elsewhere. Local authorities, voluntary school correspondents and head-teachers are none of them particularly careful or consistent either in compiling or preserving archives. Most educational historians have had the frustrating experience of finding gaps in locally kept material, only to discover more complete sets of the required documents in central records. Nor do local sources help as much as we would wish to fill out a story and bring it alive. Local minute books and reports give cold statements, not the background or heat of battle; this is probably why so much local research tends to produce records of things rather than of people. Although local decision taking is just as subject to human influence as policy making at Westminster, it has a more bureaucratic aura because the personal aspects are rarely written up. It is far easier to track down the origins of a particular policy in the cabinet room of 10 Downing Street than to attach a face to a decision taken in a town hall or local education office.

All this suggests that whilst it may be quite legitimate to write the political and administrative histories of establishments or agencies in the nineteenth and twentieth centuries (what happened can, of course, be recorded) it would be optimistic to expect them to add much to the national picture except in very special instances. But this is not to dismiss local research out of hand or to say that it is without value to the historian. There are some things which local study does poorly but others which it does well. Despite what has been said so far, there are types of information in the localities without which no large history can be written. If the overt phenomena of education are repetitious, it is important to remember that when we examine them we are looking at surface growth which is only explicable in the light of what lies underneath. Educational activity, in all its facets, is a guided response to contextual situations, some of which — perhaps the most significant — are firmly grounded in particular societies. Ready-to-hand official records, and private papers of public personages, are useful for understanding action and conduct but it is equally important to the historian to probe the spawning-grounds of the problems and movements which precede behavioural reaction. It is a tautology to say that situations can

only be explored *in situ* but this is perhaps the main value of field study
— to examine the seed and origins of what happened in the habitat
where beginnings naturally occurred. Solutions to problems, in the form
of policies and institutions, were frequently imposed from above; nineteenth-century radicals, in particular, had a leaning towards the single,
blueprint answer which, in itself, diminishes the usefulness of individual
portraits. But the problems to which the events were a response were
multiple, with wide regional differences. In the field of education there
are many aspects which have to be studied 'from below' because that is
where roots lie and where the information has to be sought.

The elementary-school question, which occupied so much of the
nineteenth century, revolved around a population explosion combined
with unprecedented urban growth; for this reason it cannot be separated
from all the other problems of housing, health and municipal development with which city dwellers had to cope. Similarly, it cannot be
isolated from commercial and industrial change or from patterns of
child labour; by the same token, theories of education are not likely to
have developed without some relation to the physical factors which
produced philosophical conflict in other social, political or economic
areas. The fact is that town-dwellers did not live in educational or
sanitary or civil-disciplinary compartments; whilst some gave greater
attention to one aspect rather than another, the environment into
which they were thrown was the sum of all problems and it is not
unusual to find that the prime movers for elementary education were
the same group of activists who were concerned in all. But there was
no single or uniform urban situation common to the whole country;
conditions varied from town to town. The needs of children crowded
into cellars in the heart of Manchester were different from those in the
small mill-towns of the Rossendale Valley or the overgrown villages
clinging to the slopes of the Pennines. The loose chaos of Liverpool or
Leeds presented child problems which were different in kind as well as
in magnitude from those of more socially compact mining communities.
Differences in locale produced differences in solutions and, also, differences in the sense of urgency with which the varying difficulties were
regarded. There are a vast number of questions here for the educational
historian. To what extent were local activists for school provision
involved in other forms of environmental improvement? Did differences
in attitude to education between one district and another correlate with
social differences between areas, not to mention variations in denominational distribution or in economic power groups? Were elementary

schools for the labouring poor a distinctively big-city problem which only gradually affected other areas? Delay in establishing a national system of schools is normally connected with religious conflict; may it not also have been related to a lack of consensus as a result of regional incohesion?

The countryside – where half of the population still lived in 1850 – presented its own contrasts and prompts another series of questions. Are we right to assume that the grass-roots of the educational revolution lay only in the cities and that the traditional method of providing for the poor through philanthropy and patronage was able to match rural aspirations even though it may have limped badly in the towns? We talk broadly about the decline in rural population but was this a fall in real numbers or only in relation to urban expansion and were there no new areas of rural growth? It is generally accepted that the countryside remained the preserve of squire and parson, but was their influence any greater than that of employer and parson in many industrial districts, particularly in company towns? And to what extent and at what point of time was the landowning interest eroded by rising standards amongst country people?

These are, of course, questions of social history but they are also fundamental to the policies of education, as was clearly appreciated at the time. In selecting regions for a sample survey of educational needs, the Newcastle Commissioners not only included contrasting urban and rural districts but broke down each of these categories in order to differentiate between types of agriculture and different kinds of industry. There is no doubt that we need a great deal more information of this sort if we are to feel confident about our explanations of national elementary education. We need to know even more about the grass-roots of local movements for bettering middle-class schools, on which surprisingly little work has been done. Nineteenth-century parliamentarians were increasingly conscious of a growing education lobby pressing for reform at all levels; to what extent did its various members act as spokesmen for organizations representative of different local interests which were themselves rooted in varying conditions? If we wish to justify the value of this type of local study we need look no further than Professor Everitt's searching probe into the ecology of rural dissent included in this volume. A surfeit of local administrative studies may, as has been suggested, be regressively rewarding, but the localities are still rich in the sort of information most able to explain, rather than to describe, what happened, not only in the districts themselves but also at the level of government.

II

The quantity of local research which is going on in the field of educational history must be very large. Much of it, however, is conducted not by trained, professional historians but by students in the colleges and departments of education, many of whom are probably beginners in the use of historical techniques. At this level, local studies are a significant growth industry. Students are pegging out the land like Sacramento Valley, eagerly digging and sifting their particular territory. Since each claim can be bounded by chronological as well as geographical limits, and can be worked separately at primary, secondary or tertiary levels, it is clear that there is work for all for a long time to come. The period between 1870 and 1903 alone yields upwards of 2,500 school boards, each of which can be turned over and panned. Employment seems secure.

There seem to be three main reasons for this student activity. To begin with, what occurs on the ground can be studied on the ground. Macro-policy might be formulated at Westminster but the educational process itself takes place in schools and colleges. Education is a matter of pupils and teachers, of buildings and facilities. These exist and interact (together with local policy-makers and machinery for local policy-making) not as a single, planned landscape but as a multiplicity of variegated clumps. If we want a student to know what it was like to be in an elementary school in 1850, and why the school was like it was, it is obviously rewarding for him to look at particular schools and what happened in them.

Secondly, a local study is thought to be a useful training exercise in the handling of records. The assumption here is that contact with contemporary material imparts realism. This, at least, is an assumption dear to teachers of history although its validity has never been clearly demonstrated. For more advanced students it is believed, no doubt rightly, that insight into the nature of history is enriched by active involvement in the creation of a piece of history. The nature of evidence, what we mean by a 'historical fact' and the construction of generalizations can best be learned by a do-it-yourself method, and a local study is generally thought to provide a convenient and uncomplex training ground.

The third reason is that localities, like Mount Everest, are there, waiting to be explored, with the great advantage over Mount Everest that they always happen to be on some student's doorstep.

All these are good reasons and what follows is a comment, not on the desirability of research into local educational history, but on the way in which some student exercises seem to be conducted. It is questionable whether the actual results are really commensurate with the immense activity which is going on.

Some time ago I asked a candidate for a senior post in a college of education why he had never followed a course of higher study in education. He replied that he could, of course, have written an historical account of the Oswaldtwistle School Board for an M.Ed. degree but it had been more productive for him, as a person, to concentrate what time and energy he had on his own teaching. This struck home. As one who has had to read many scores of theses on Oswaldtwistle School Boards, Bumpington School Boards and secondary education in a plethora of Humpingtons, I long since came to the conclusion that, with few exceptions, when you have read one you have read them all. By and large, they are not interpretative studies but, in the term used by the man I interviewed, 'accounts' or compilations of factual data, carefully extracted from whatever records were available, structured chronologically or thematically, but usually nothing more than a display of items rather than attempts at explanation. The poorer efforts exhibit lack of discrimination and throw in every piece of researched material. The better productions are less inclusive of educational detail. They usually open with selected topographical and sociological information designed as a backcloth to set a scene and help understanding, before they too settle down to lay out the store of gathered facts — sometimes with little attempt to connect the goods exhibited on the stage with the backcloth behind.

This is not to revive the controversy between the cult of facts and those who believe that history is philosophy. There is probably no clear-cut polarization between the two schools. But most historians would accept that mere accumulation of the data (and, too often, of the jumble and debris) of history is antiquarianism and does not, by itself, constitute worthwhile historical scholarship. Work done by students up to, and including, master's-degree level may sometimes cross new frontiers and contribute new dimensions to knowledge. If it does, this is a bonus. But normally, the object of teaching and research into educational history is to educate the student — to deepen his insight into the factors which have, historically, influenced the theory and practice of education and to further his own training in scholarship. If this is true of research exercises in general, it is difficult to find an excuse for exempting localized investigations from the normal rule. The value of a local study should be assessed on the same criteria which we apply to other studies; that is to say, it should be judged by the contribution which it makes to the student's education, by which we mean the expansion of his experience and insights.

We have to ask if the investigator who ploughs a lonely way through local data, classifying his results with sensible ingenuity, is likely to acquire greater insights into the forces, pressures and development of educational history than he would obtain from reading Seaborne on Leicester, the Simons on Leicestershire or Wardle on Nottingham, simply because he pursues an active method of learning by discovery. For the very good student, who brings with him considerable comprehension of trends and concepts on which to build, there will undoubtedly be gain. For the ordinary run-of-the-mill student I am not so sure. I think that we underestimate the amount of pre-knowledge which is necessary for understanding and interpreting local data. I have never been convinced by the logic which assumes that a happening in our own backyard is by nature more commonplace or less sophisticated than one which takes place a hundred miles away in someone else's backyard. We still have to learn to walk before running even if our sole intention is to sprint round the local park. It is just as necessary to know what we are looking for and to recognize what we find whether we are going through Cabinet papers or visitation returns.

In a recent thesis presented for a master's degree the writer recorded that in the nineteenth-century industrial locale that he was examining, elementary schools were provided far more generously by Roman Catholics than by Anglicans. This, he assumed in passing, was because Catholics were wealthier than Anglicans. It seemed to him a logical explanation. It is however a startling assertion. The writer was clearly unaware that Catholic communities in Lancashire towns (and it was one of these with which he was dealing) were normally made up of low-income workers, mainly Irish immigrants, without a middle-class leaven. If he was reading and recording his facts correctly he had therefore stumbled on an oddity which needed far more investigation than he gave it. By failing to recognize this he missed an opportunity. More serious is the suspicion that because he was insufficiently grounded in his subject he misled himself, on the basis of a single instance, into accepting the untenable theory that all Catholic communities were affluent. So far from furthering his appreciation of historical development, the method of learning by discovery had mistaught him.

The recorder of yet another area noted that his own particular school board was urged by H.M.I., in 1894, to concentrate all its higher standards in a single school. Here is a real nugget — an instance of official pressure for Hadow reorganization in the 1890s. But to the writer it was just one more pebble to join the heap. He only mentioned it, in fact, to illustrate that the school board was not particularly interested in what went on inside schools and preferred to leave pedagogical matters to H.M.I.

A good illustration of the risks that beginners run when they are left free to dig a plot for themselves is the way in which students have been known to treat nonconformist provision of elementary schools in the nineteenth century. There is a recognizable pattern. Writers devote a chapter to recording the number of schools erected, the dates and cost of erection, the number of children accommodated, the location of the schools — with map — the size and qualifications of staff, and so on; then come a couple of sentences at the end excusing the relative paucity of provision on the grounds that dissenters could not, in any case, compete with the Church of the Establishment which they assume to be, by definition, the Church of wealth and privilege. This is, of course, an example of textbook orthodoxy which probably has little national validity and cannot possibly be true of every area. It assumes a universality which transcends the particular. If nonconformists were not always the poorer section of the community (and, in fact, some dissenting sects — the Congregationalists, for example — were amongst the wealthiest) other factors must be sought to explain dissenting inertia. But to record the results of inactivity and use a bromide to interpret them, instead of probing the facts to test the bromide, bypasses the real purpose of local investigation and adds nothing to a student's stature.

I am not blaming students for being unequipped to cope with their material. I wonder, however, whether noting information without recognizing or exploring its significance can be said to advance their education. What I am questioning is not the value of local investigations but the belief that they are relatively uncomplicated and can be profitably undertaken by beginners.

But even if the student fails to make the most of his material, might he not gain in scholarship by carrying out an exercise in historical method? The answer must be 'yes' provided that he employs historical method and is not just locating sources, annotating them and classifying the results. Research implies asking questions and finding answers. It means defining specific problems and seeking material to illuminate them; or postulating hypotheses and testing them against documented evidence. A student who works along these lines will gain experience of scientific method because he will be using it. But if his coverage is ill-defined or diffuse he gains little. If he sets off to review the work of the Extown school board or grammar school provision in the north-eastern end of the county of Whyshire with no particular questions in mind he may turn up suggestive clues which later and better-equipped expeditions might follow up (there is a chicken-and-egg syndrome here) but he learns little about a scientific approach to research. Indiscriminate forays into local sectors are often defended on the grounds that they are moon-probes, bringing back material which the real experts can examine at leisure. To employ students as laboratory assistants may or may not be justifiable but we should not claim to be training them in research if all they are doing is setting up the apparatus.

Local investigations do, of course, have purpose. There are some problems which only occur in a particular terrain. The difficulties of providing schools in a sparsely populated area must be studied in just such an area. Montgomeryshire might be a suitable choice but the object of the study would not be to put Montgomeryshire in the bag of counties about which we have a local history but to identify the problems of sparsity and the way in which they were tackled in that particular county. That is to say, the information that Montgomeryshire provides should be used functionally to give answers to questions. In the same way, in his work on what he calls the 'crucial experiment' in elementary education [3], Dr Murphy took a unique incident in Liverpool and examined it in its appropriate context; the subject had its imperial documentation but could only be understood in its native situation.

It is well-known that higher-grade schools came to be used by certain groups of middle-class children although it is supposed that they were intended, in concept, for the working class; they are, indeed, often projected as a brave and progressive effort on the part of forward-looking school boards to extend working-class opportunity. A recent study of higher-grade schools in Manchester, however, shows that in that city they were conceived as middle-class schools from the outset, conveniently and deliberately located to serve a middle-class population. This suggests that they did not just become Grade III secondary schools but were planned as such; that they represented a continuity of the practice, deplored by Newcastle and Lowe, of diverting to middle-class purposes funds which were provided for the labouring poor; and that higher-grade schools in the 1870s might have been the direct consequence of Forster's inability to force through the provision of rate-aid to middle-class education in 1869, coupled with the return of a Conservative Government in 1874. There are a number of hypotheses here which need examining and can only be tested by specific in-depth studies in appropriate localities, to see if what was true of Manchester held good elsewhere. Pieces of work of this nature are well within the capacity of students. They imply local inquiries, but inquiries with a purpose. The localities are a mine of information but random digging is not particularly productive. The yield is always far more satisfying when we use them as a source of required information because they are the natural deposit-ground of the material for which we are searching.

To sum up, there is no doubt that localized investigations have an important part to play in historical research and a serious contribution to make to historical knowledge. This is not in question. For the students in our colleges and departments, however, their value is more problematical and in setting them to work it may be desirable to keep four points in mind:

(1)   Research investigations undertaken by students should be considered as part of their education and training;
(2)   Exploring a locality can be as full of pitfalls for beginners as many national studies;
(3)   Local research is only useful as an exercise in historiography insofar as it employs historical method;
(4)   Local studies, like other well-conducted educational exercises, are most valuable when they are purposeful, when we are searching a particular piece of ground because we know what we are looking for and have reason to suppose that we will find it in a chosen locality.

Notes

1   M.E. Bryant, review article, *Journal of Educational Administration and History* (Leeds, December 1971), p. 62.
2   See C. Bardsley, 'Secondary Education in Stockport', unpublished M.Ed. thesis (Manchester, 1963).
3   J. Murphy, *The Religious Problem in English Education: the Crucial Experiment* (Liverpool, 1959).

Index